PEP GUARI
ATTACKING TACTICS

Tactical Analysis and Sessions from Manchester City's 4-3-3

WRITTEN BY
ATHANASIOS TERZIS

PUBLISHED BY

PEP GUARDIOLA ATTACKING TACTICS

Tactical Analysis and Sessions from Manchester City's 4-3-3

First Published May 2019 by SoccerTutor.com

info@soccertutor.com | www.SoccerTutor.com

UK: 0208 1234 007 | **US:** (305) 767 4443 | **ROTW:** +44 208 1234 007

ISBN: 978-1-910491-31-7

Author

Athanasios Terzis © 2019

Edited by

Alex Fitzgerald - SoccerTutor.com

Cover Design by

Alex Macrides, Think Out Of The Box Ltd.
Email: design@thinkootb.com Tel: +44 (0) 208 144 3550

Diagrams

Diagram designs by SoccerTutor.com. All the diagrams in this book have been created using SoccerTutor.com Tactics Manager Software available from www.SoccerTutor.com

Note: While every effort has been made to ensure the technical accuracy of the content of this book, neither the author nor publishers can accept any responsibility for any injury or loss sustained as a result of the use of this material.

CONTENTS

PEP GUARDIOLA'S ATTACKING TACTICS

MEET THE AUTHOR: ATHANASIOS TERZIS

- **UEFA 'A' Coaching Licence**

- **M.S.C. in Coaching and Conditioning**

- **Greek Football Federation Instructor (HFF)**

- **Former Coach of Professional Teams in Greece**

- **Former Coach of Semi-Pro Teams in Greece**

- **Former Technical Director of DOXA Dramas Academy** (Greek 2nd division)

- **Former Professional Football Player**

Athanasios Terzis is a football tactics expert and is regularly invited as an instructor to many coaching seminars and workshops around the world.

Athanasios has written many successful football coaching books published by **SoccerTutor.com**, which have sold thousands of copies worldwide in multiple languages (English, Spanish, German, Italian, Greek, Japanese, Korean and Chinese):

- **Creative Attacking Play - From the Tactics of Conte, Allegri, Simeone, Mourinho, Wenger & Klopp** (2017)

- **Marcelo Bielsa - Coaching Build Up Play Against High Pressing Teams** (2017)

- **Coaching the Juventus 3-5-2 - Tactical Analysis and Sessions: Attacking and Defending** (2016)

- **Jürgen Klopp's Attacking and Defending Tactics: Tactical Analysis and Sessions from Borussia Dortmund's 4-2-3-1** (2015)

- **FC Barcelona Training Sessions: 160 Practices from 34 Tactical Situations** (2013)
  * Winner of Italian FA Award for "Best Coaching Book" 2014

- **Jose Mourinho's Real Madrid - A Tactical Analysis: Attacking and Defending in the 4-2-3-1** (2012)

- **FC Barcelona - A Tactical Analysis: Attacking and Defending** (2012)

PEP GUARDIOLA'S ACHIEVEMENTS

COACHING ROLES

- **Manchester City** (2016 - Present)
- **Bayern Munich** (2013 - 2016)
- **Barcelona** (2008 - 2012)
- **Barcelona B** (2007 - 2008)

HONOURS (Europe/World)

- **UEFA Champions League x 2** (2009, 2011)
- **FIFA Club World Cup x 3** (2009, 2011, 2013)
- **UEFA Super Cup x 3** (2009, 2011, 2013)

HONOURS (Domestic Leagues)

- **English Premier League x 2** (2018, 2019)
- **German Bundesliga x 3** (2014, 2015, 2016)
- **Spanish La Liga x 3** (2009, 2010, 2011)
- **Spanish Tercera (2nd) División** (2008)

HONOURS (Domestic Cups)

- **English FA Cup** (2019)
- **German DFB-Pokal x 2** (2014, 2016)
- **Spanish Copa del Rey x 2** (2009, 2012)
- **English EFL Cup x 2** (2018, 2019)
- **Spanish Supercopa de España x 3** (2009, 2010, 2011)

INDIVIDUAL AWARDS

- **FIFA World Coach of the Year** (2011)
- **European Coach of Season - Press Association** (2011)
- **European Coach of Year - Alf Ramsey Award** (2009)
- **English Premier League Manager of Season** (2018)
- **La Liga Coach of the Year x 4** (2009, 2010, 2011, 2012)

MANCHESTER CITY'S TROPHIES AND RECORDS (2017-2019)

2017-2018

Premier League

EFL Cup

In the 2017-2018 season, Pep Guardiola's Manchester City team won the Premier League title and the EFL Cup. They achieved this while breaking 8 all-time Premier League Records (*):

* Highest Ever Points Total (100 Points) *
* Most Total Wins (32) *
* Most Goals Scored (106) *
* Most Away Wins (16) *
* Biggest Goal Difference (+79) *
* Biggest Title-Winning Margin (19 Points) *
* Most Consecutive Wins (18) *
* Fewest Minutes Trailing/Losing (153 min) *

2018-2019

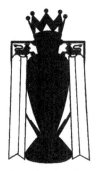

Premier League

FA Cup

EFL Cup

In the 2018-2019 season, Pep Guardiola's Manchester City team retained the Premier League title, maintaining their very high standards by equalling their **Most Total Wins Record (32)***, amounting **98 Points**, scoring **95 Goals**, getting **14 Away Wins** and registering a **+72 Goal Difference**.

They also won the FA Cup and the EFL Cup, landing a **Domestic Treble** and broke the following records:

* **First English Top-Flight Team to Win Every Major English Trophy in a Single Season (Community Shield, EFL Cup, FA Cup and Premier League)**
* **Most Goals in All Competitions for an English Top-Flight Team (163)**
* **Equalled All-Time Record for FA Cup Final Winning Margin (6-0 vs Watford)**
 - Set by Bury's 6-0 Win vs Derby in 1903.

* Trophy images from **PIXSECTOR.com**

PEP GUARDIOLA'S MANCHESTER CITY FORMATION (4-3-3)

Manchester City's 4-3-3 Formation

Pep Guardiola's Manchester City mainly use the 4-3-3 formation.

However, there were some matches where Pep adapted and used the 4-2-3-1 or the 3-5-2 formation. However, this book will focus on how the 4-3-3 was implemented.

Manchester City's 4-3-3 Formation (Squad Players)

This diagram shows the other players that were involved for Manchester City at different times during the 2017-2018 and 2018-2019 seasons.

Bernardo (20) was an ever-present during the 2018-2019 season and **Gündoğan (8)** also played many games mainly as an attacking midfielder, and sometimes as the defensive midfielder.

Stones (5) and **Kompany (4)** played many games at centre back.

PEP GUARDIOLA'S 2-3-2-3 ATTACKING FORMATION

Manchester City's 2-3-2-3 Attacking Formation

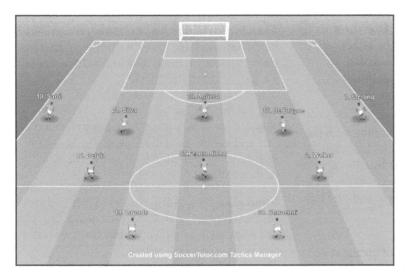

During the attacking phase, the formation changed to 2-3-2-3, which created 4 lines of players.

This helped the team move the ball gradually from the 2 centre backs to the players in more advanced positions (either wide or centrally).

This was very interesting as the positioning of both full backs was central (inverted) instead of wide.

Manchester City's 2-3-2-3 Attacking Formation (Squad Players)

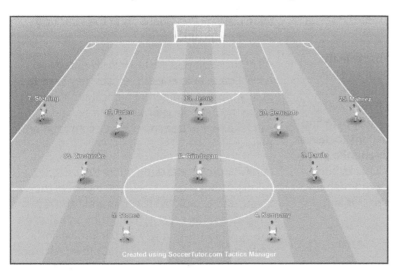

This diagram shows the 2-3-2-3 attacking formation with other players that were involved for Manchester City at different times during the 2017-2018 and 2018-2019 seasons.

THE MANCHESTER CITY PLAYERS

GOALKEEPER

Ederson is very adept at taking part in Manchester City's build up play. **Ederson's** ability to use his feet with accuracy in the attacking phase fits perfectly with Pep Guardiola's demands in building up play from the back.

CENTRE BACKS

Laporte (14) and **Stones (5)** are better with the ball and have the ability to dribble it forward with ease, while **Otamendi (30)** and the captain **Kompany (4)** are stronger at defending, while at the same time still being adequate with the ball.

FULL BACKS

Walker (2) played the majority of games at right back throughout the 2017/2018 and 2018/2019 seasons, while **Delph (18)**, **Zinchenko (35)** and sometimes **Laporte (14)** or **Danilo (3)** were used at left back. It should be mentioned that **Mendy (22)** was unavailable for long periods due to injury problems.

Pep Guardiola uses inverted full backs in the attacking phase (2-3-2-3 formation) and wants technically gifted players in the full back positions. **Walker (2)** uses his ability, speed and stamina to continuously make overlapping and mainly underlapping runs on the flank to deliver crosses, while **Delph (18)** and **Zinchenko (35)** act more like midfielders than full backs from their central positions. However, both of them have the ability to play accurate passes and deliver quality early crosses.

DEFENSIVE MIDFIELDER

Fernandinho (25) is perfect for this role as he has the ability to read the game and takes up the appropriate positioning for any tactical situation. His contribution across both the 2017/2018 and 2018/2019 seasons was outstanding and he is a key player for this Manchester City side.

Apart from his effective positioning which always made him available to receive potential passes from the defenders, **Fernandinho (25)** also has a big role during the attacking phase. He can play through balls to the attacking midfielders and the forward, as well as switch play to the wingers - he is very adept at helping his team find and exploit available spaces. The Brazilian international also often finds himself in positions to shoot at goal.

Gündoğan (8) was also chosen to play in this position for Pep Guardiola's Manchester City, but this was mainly when **Fernandinho (25)** was unavailable or being rested.

ATTACKING MIDFIELDERS

Silva (21), **De Bruyne (17)**, **Bernardo (20)**, **Gündoğan (8)** and occasionally **Foden (47)** were used by Pep Guardiola in the attacking midfielder positions.

All of these players are technically gifted and have a great awareness of space. They have the ability to read all different tactical situations, make the right decisions in a split second and can take part in fast and decisive combination play.

Pep Guardiola's attacking midfielders display good positioning and tactical awareness to create and exploit overloads in wide areas, play key passes after receiving and turning between the opposition's midfield and defensive lines, make well-timed diagonal runs, provide accurate low crosses, early crosses and are adept at shooting from central positions.

WINGERS

Sané (19), **Sterling (7)**, **Bernardo (20)** and **Mahrez (26)** were played as wingers, with **Sterling (7)** playing the majority of games.

All of these players are skilful at speed and are very capable of beating their opponents in different 1v1 situations when the opposing full backs were isolated.

They also used well-timed runs to receive through balls in behind opposing full backs and deliver accurate low crosses.

A frequent attacking move for Pep Guardiola's Manchester City included the wingers cutting inside after passing to a player positioned centrally. This movement was exploited with a 1-2 combination or with a give-and-go and ended with the winger receiving in a favourable position inside the penalty area, ready to either deliver a low cross or shoot at goal.

FORWARD

Agüero (10) and **Jesus (33)** were picked by Pep Guardiola for the forward role. These 2 skilful forwards are very good at playing in tight spaces and scoring goals under limited time and space.

They frequently use diagonal runs to receive in behind the opposition's defence and take up appropriate positions in order to finish on goal after a low or early cross. Even though neither player is tall, they are able to score several goals with their heads due to their good positioning.

Their contribution was very important in providing the finishing touches, but they also played an important role in the build up and creating chances. They dropped back between the lines to offer passing options to **Fernandinho (25)** or the full backs, and often acted as link players to move the ball to the attacking midfielders.

KEY PLAYER STATISTICS (ALL COMPETITIONS)

2017-2018 SEASON

- **Agüero: 30 Goals / 7 Assists**
- **Sterling: 23 Goals / 17 Assists**
- **Jesus: 17 Goals / 5 Assists**
- **Sané: 14 Goals / 19 Assists**
- **De Bruyne: 12 Goals / 21 Assists**
- **Silva: 10 Goals / 14 Assists**
- **Bernardo: 9 Goals / 11 Assists**
- **Gündoğan: 6 Goals / 7 Assists**
- **Fernandinho: 5 Goals / 5 Assists**

2018-2019 SEASON

- **Agüero: 32 Goals / 10 Assists**
- **Sterling: 25 Goals / 18 Assists**
- **Jesus: 21 Goals / 6 Assists**
- **Sané: 16 Goals / 18 Assists**
- **Bernardo: 13 Goals / 13 Assists**
- **Mahrez: 12 Goals / 12 Assists**
- **Silva: 10 Goals / 14 Assists**
- **De Bruyne: 6 Goals / 11 Assists**
- **Gündoğan: 6 Goals / 8 Assists**

INTRODUCTION

Apart from his success in winning trophies, Pep Guardiola is admired for his spectacular attacking style of play. All the teams he has coached have been wonderful to watch:

- **Manchester City** (2016 - Present)
- **Bayern Munich** (2013 - 2016)
- **Barcelona** (2008 - 2012)

This book goes into great depth on Manchester City's attacking style under Pep Guardiola (especially in the final third) during the 2017-2018 and 2018-2019 Premier League winning seasons.

The attacking phase is the phase during which the team is in possession of the ball and includes all the actions taken in order to create scoring chances and score goals.

The following key tactical elements are covered in this book with extensive analysis and full training sessions for how to coach each specific tactical situation:

- **TACTICAL SITUATION 1:**
  Overcoming the Pressing of the Opposing Forwards

- **TACTICAL SITUATION 2:**
  Positioning and Rotations with Inverted Full Backs

- **TACTICAL SITUATION 3:**
  Creating and Exploiting Overloads in Wide Areas

- **TACTICAL SITUATION 4:**
  Attacking Options when the Overload Out Wide is Blocked

- **TACTICAL SITUATION 5:**
  Moving the Ball Wide and Receiving in Behind the Full Back (or Create Space for Inside Pass)

- **TACTICAL SITUATION 6:**
  Combination Play Out Wide when the Overload is Blocked

- **TACTICAL SITUATION 7:**
  Stretching the Opposition's Defence and Switching Play

- **TACTICAL SITUATION 8:**
  Attacking Options when the Attacking Midfielder Receives Between the Lines

- **TACTICAL SITUATION 9:**
  Exploiting Space Created when the Opposing Centre Back Pushes Out to Press the Ball

- **TACTICAL SITUATION 10:**
  Attacking Through the Centre with the Forward Dropping Back to Receive

- **TACTICAL SITUATION 11:**
  Switching Play to the Weak Side when the Overload is Blocked Against the 4-3-3

- **TACTICAL SITUATION 12:**
  Attacking Against a Back 5

COACHING FORMAT

1. TACTICAL SITUATION AND ANALYSIS

- The analysis is based on recurring patterns of play observed within **Pep Guardiola's Manchester City** team. Once the same phase of play occurred a number of times (at least 10), the tactics would be seen as a pattern.

- Each action, pass, individual movement (with or without the ball) and the positioning of each player on the pitch including their body shape, are presented with a full description.

2. TRAINING SESSION BASED ON THE TACTICS OF PEP GUARDIOLA

- Technical and Functional Unopposed Practices
- Functional and Tactical Opposed Practices
- Small Sided Games / Conditioned Games
- Name/Objective and Full Description
- Conditions, Progressions, Variations & Coaching Points (if applicable)

KEY

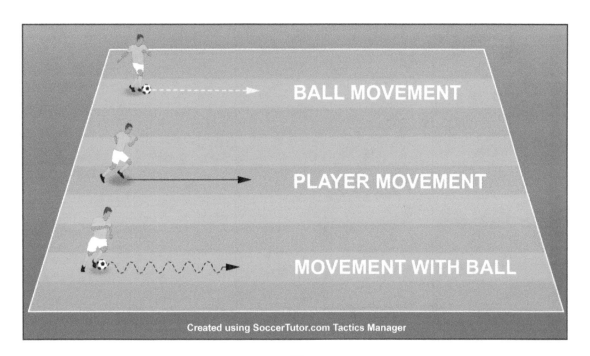

Created using SoccerTutor.com Tactics Manager

ATTACKING AGAINST THE 4-4-2 OR 4-2-3-1

ATTACKING AGAINST THE 4-4-2 OR 4-2-3-1

As already mentioned, the attacking formation of Manchester City changes to 2-3-2-3 and Pep Guardiola's philosophy in the attacking phase is based on moving the ball gradually through the lines.

When playing against the 4-4-2 or the 4-2-3-1, the centre backs **(14 & 30)** aimed to move the ball to the 3 players in front of them in the next line. These are the inverted full backs **(35 & 2)** and the defensive midfielder **(25)**, who take up positions between the opposition's forward and midfield lines.

The full backs or defensive midfielder most often then move the ball to an attacking midfielder **(21 & 17)**. However, the ball was also sometimes moved directly to a winger **(19 & 7)** or the forward **(10)**, who dropped back between the opposition's midfield and defensive lines.

The next phase for the Manchester City players is to attack in the final third, playing key passes, crossing into the penalty area or shooting at goal.

1. Spaces Available and Passing Options for Second Line Players to Receive from the Centre Backs (Against the 4-4-2)

Available space for City players to receive

Created using SoccerTutor.com Tactics Manager

When playing against the 4-4-2, the 3 target players **(35, 25 & 2 in the second line)** move towards the available spaces, which are created according to the positioning of the opposing forwards and midfielders, while also retaining their shape.

There is available space on the right and left for the full backs **(35 & 2)** to exploit, as well as some space in the centre for the defensive midfielder **Fernandinho (25)** to receive.

2. Spaces Available and Passing Options for Second Line Players to Receive from the Centre Backs (Against the 4-2-3-1)

Available space for City players to receive

Created using SoccerTutor.com Tactics Manager

When playing against the 4-2-3-1, the space in the centre for the defensive midfielder **Fernandinho (25)** was restricted by the opposing No.10.

This meant that **Fernandinho (25)** couldn't receive a direct pass from the centre backs most of the time, so they would play to the inverted full backs instead **(35 & 2)**.

TACTICAL SITUATION 1

Overcoming the Pressing of the Opposing Forwards

Content from Analysis of Manchester City during the 2017/2018 and 2018/2019 Premier League winning seasons

The analysis is based on recurring patterns of play observed within the Manchester City team. Once the same phase of play occurred a number of times (at least 10) the tactics would be seen as a pattern. The analysis on the next page is an example of the team's tactics being used effectively, taken from a specific game.

Each action, pass, individual movement with or without the ball, and the positioning of each player on the pitch including their body shape, are presented.

The analysis is then used to create a full progressive session to coach this specific tactical situation.

OVERCOMING THE PRESSING OF THE OPPOSING FORWARDS

When the opposing forward/s tried to put pressure on the centre backs or the inverted full backs in a way which forced the ball wide, they were attempting to create a strong side to trap the Manchester City players and win possession. Pep Guardiola's side had the solutions, which we show in this section.

1. Overcoming the Pressing of the Opposing Forward on the Centre Back Using a Link Player (Against the 4-4-2)

The red forward (No.10) moves quickly towards the City centre back **Kompany (4)** to force him to play wide (to full back) and create a strong side for his team to apply effective pressing. Pep Guardiola's City players find a way to move the ball to the other side by using link players.

In this example, the attacking midfielder **Gündoğan (8)** drops deep, offers a passing option and becomes the link player to move the ball to the defensive midfielder **Fernandinho (25)**, who is free and has many passing options to players in space **(35, 17, 19 & 10)**.

2. Overcoming the Pressing of the Opposing Forward on the Full Back **Using a Link Player** (Against the 4-4-2)

In a similar situation to the previous example, the red forward (10) moves to press the right back **Walker (2)**.

Red No.10's aim is to force **Walker (2)** to play wide to the right winger **Sterling (7)** and then apply pressing with 3 red players (3, 8 & 11).

With red No.10 restricting the immediate available space, City again use the attacking midfielder **Gündoğan (8)** as a link player.

As soon as the red forward (10) moves to press the right back **Walker (2)**, the attacking midfielder **Gündoğan (8)** drops into an effective position to offer a passing option and become a link player.

Gündoğan (8) passes back to the defensive midfielder **Fernandinho (25)**.

Fernandinho (25) receives free in space in the centre and has many passing options to players in space **(35, 17, 19 & 10)**.

3. Overcoming the Pressing of the Opposing Forward on the Centre Back **Using a Link Player** (Against the 4-2-3-1)

Against the 4-2-3-1 formation, the defensive midfielder **Fernandinho (25)** was most often restricted by the opposing No.10.

This meant that the potential pass of a link player would not be directed to **Fernandinho (25)**. Instead, the link player would play back to the centre back on the weak side, which is **Stones (5)** in the diagram example.

The red forward (No.9) moves quickly towards the Manchester City centre back **Kompany (4)** to force him to play wide (to full back) and create a strong side for his team to apply effective pressing.

As he did against the 4-4-2 formation, the attacking midfielder **Gündoğan (8)** drops deep, offers a passing option and becomes the link player. This time, he passes back to **Stones (5)**, who is the centre back on the weak side.

Stones (5) is free and passes to the full back on the other side **Zinchenko (35)**, who can pass to the attacking midfielder **De Bruyne (17)** or the winger **Sané (19)** on the weak side.

4. Overcoming the Pressing of the Opposing Forward on the Full Back Using a Link Player (Against the 4-2-3-1)

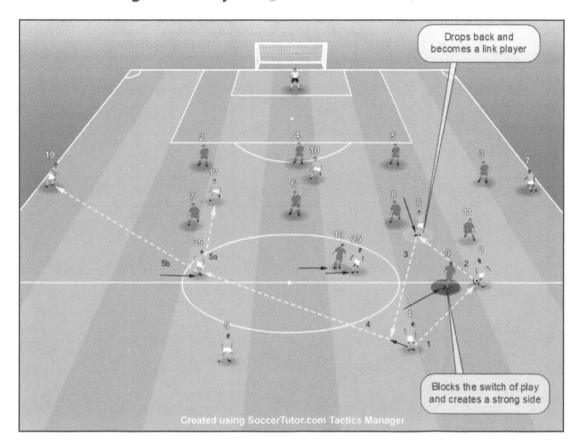

In a similar situation to the previous example, the red forward (No.9) moves to press the right back **Walker (2)**.

Red No.10's aim is to force **Walker (2)** to play wide to the right winger **Sterling (7)** and then apply pressing with 3 red players (3, 8 & 11).

With red No.10 restricting the immediate available space, City again use the attacking midfielder **Gündoğan (8)** as a link player.

As soon as the red forward (No.9) moves to press the right back **Walker (2)**, the attacking midfielder **Gündoğan (8)** drops into an effective position to offer a passing option and become a link player.

Gündoğan (8) this time directs the ball back to the centre back **Kompany (4)**, who is left unmarked and free in space to receive.

Kompany (4) receives and passes to the full back on the other side **Zinchenko (35)**, who can pass to the attacking midfielder **De Bruyne (17)** or the winger **Sané (19)** on the weak side.

5. Overcoming the Pressing of the Opposing Forward on the Defensive Midfielder **Using a Link Player** (Against the 4-4-2)

In this final tactical example, **Fernandinho (25)** receives from the centre back **Kompany (4)** and is put under pressure by the opposing forward (red No.9).

In this situation, the forward **Agüero (10)** drops back to become the link player and passes back to left back **Zinchenko (35)**, who is unmarked.

NOTE:

This situation with the defensive midfielder **Fernandinho (25)** being pressed by a forward mostly happened against the 4-4-2 formation.

When playing against the 4-2-3-1, the positioning of the opposing No.10 prevented **Fernandinho (25)** receiving from the centre backs when building up play.

Overcoming the Pressing of the Opposing Forwards

SESSION FOR THIS TACTICAL SITUATION (2 PRACTICES)

Practice 1: Overcoming the Pressing of the Opposing Forwards in a Tactical Pattern of Play

Scenario A: Attacking Midfielder Drops Back to Become Link Player

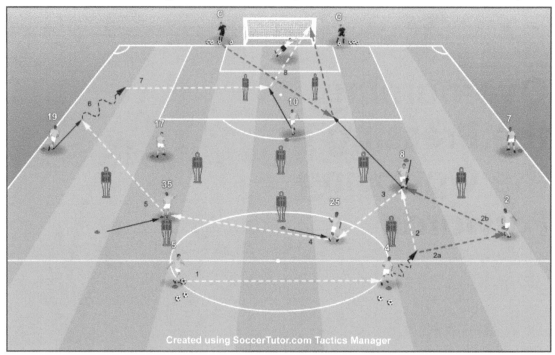

Created using SoccerTutor.com Tactics Manager

Objective: Overcoming forwards' pressing and moving the ball to the weak side.

Description (Scenario A)

The players start on the blue cones and one centre back **(No.5 in diagram)** passes to the other **(No.4)**.

The centre back who receives the first pass **(4)** dribbles the ball forward towards the closest mannequin and passes to the attacking midfielder **(No.8 in diagram)**, who drops back to act as a link player to move the ball to the defensive midfielder **(25)**.

Another option for the centre back **(4)** is to pass to the full back **(2)** and the full back passes to the attacking midfielder **(8)** - see blue arrows.

The defensive midfielder **(25)** directs the ball to a player on the weak side **(left back -35 in diagram)**, who then passes to the winger **(19)**.

The winger **(19)** dribbles the ball forward and crosses for the forward **(10)**, while the attacking midfielder **(8)** makes a run forward to support.

The forward **(10)** shoots and immediately after, the attacking midfielder **(8)** receives a pass from the coach (2nd ball) from the end line to finish.

The practice restarts with the pattern carried out on the opposite side. There can be 2 players in each position for the 5 advanced players to keep the practice running at a high tempo.

Scenario B: Forward Drops Back to Become Link Player

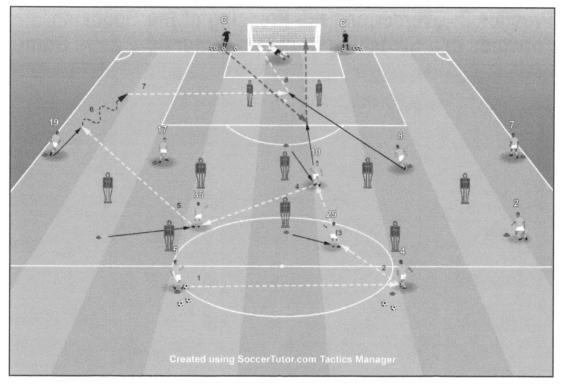

Created using SoccerTutor.com Tactics Manager

Description (Scenario B)

In Scenario B, the centre back **(4)** receives but does not dribble forward. Instead, he passes directly to the defensive midfielder **(25)**.

For Scenario B, the forward becomes the link player to move the ball to the weak side full back **(35)**, who then plays to the winger **(19)**.

The practice restarts with the pattern carried out on the opposite side.

There can be 2 players in each position for the 5 advanced players to keep the practice running at a high tempo.

Coaching Points

1. Accurate and high speed passing.

2. Well-timed movements of the players who drop back to receive (attacking midfielder or forward).

3. Accurate crossing and finishing.

PROGRESSION

Practice 2: Overcoming the Pressing of the Opposing Forwards and Switching Play in a Dynamic 2 Zone Game

Created using SoccerTutor.com Tactics Manager

Objective: Overcoming forwards' pressing and moving the ball to the weak side.

Description

The marked out area is divided vertically into 2 equal halves.

The practice starts with the coach's pass to one of the blue centre backs **(4 or 5)**.

As soon as the pass is played, the closest red forward (No.10 in diagram example) presses the receiver **(4)** and tries to create a strong side for his team. The red team's aim is to force play towards the side-line and create a numerical advantage (5 v 6) in that area of the pitch.

If the reds win the ball, they then try to score in either of the mini goals within 8 – 12 seconds.

The aim for the blues is either:

1. Find a way to score on the strong side with a numerical disadvantage (5 v 6).

2. The BEST OPTION is to move the ball to the other half (switch play to the weak side), exploit the numerical advantage there and then score.

The attacking midfielder drops back at the right moment **(No.8 in diagram example)** and is the key player to achieve a successful switch of play.

TACTICAL SITUATION 2

Positioning and Rotations with Inverted Full Backs

Content from Analysis of Manchester City during the 2017/2018 and 2018/2019 Premier League winning seasons

The analysis is based on recurring patterns of play observed within the Manchester City team. Once the same phase of play occurred a number of times (at least 10) the tactics would be seen as a pattern. The analysis on the next page is an example of the team's tactics being used effectively, taken from a specific game.

Each action, pass, individual movement with or without the ball, and the positioning of each player on the pitch including their body shape, are presented.

The analysis is then used to create a full progressive session to coach this specific tactical situation.

POSITIONING AND ROTATIONS WITH INVERTED FULL BACKS

Full Backs Move Towards the Inside when the Attacking Midfielders Take Up Advanced Positions Between the Lines

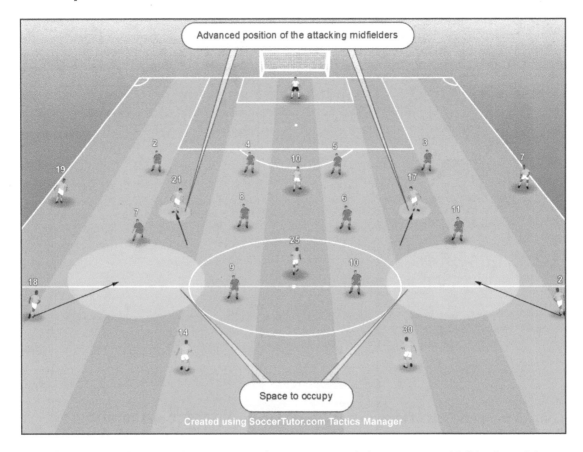

One of Pep Guardiola's tactical innovations is the use of inverted full backs, which he also used at Bayern Munich.

During the attacking phase, both full backs **(18 & 2)** move towards the inside into more central positions and create a line of 3 with the defensive midfielder **Fernandinho (25)** - this forms the second line of the team in a 2-3-2-3 attacking phase formation.

Pep Guardiola uses Inverted full backs with his Manchester City team during certain tactical situations against all possible formations.

The full backs **Delph (18)** and **Walker (2)** move towards the inside when the attacking midfielders are positioned high up and beyond the opposition's midfield line, as shown with **Silva (21)** and **De Bruyne (17)** in the diagram.

THE BENEFITS OF INVERTED FULL BACKS AND THEIR CENTRAL POSITIONING

1. Creating Triangle Shapes with Inverted Full Backs

The central positioning of the full backs provided Manchester City with several benefits.

First of all, an effective triangle shape could be formed between the full back, winger and attacking midfielder, as shown in the diagram.

2. Creating a Double Triangle with Full Back in Possession

In situations when the full back was in possession, the forward **(10)** would often drop into a deep position between the lines.

Manchester City could then create a double triangle, providing the full back **(18)** with many passing options, as shown in the diagram.

3. The Central Position of the Defensive Midfielder Enables Effective Attacking Shapes to be Created

Potential deep position of the forward

Created using SoccerTutor.com Tactics Manager

Another important benefit of using inverted full backs was that the defensive midfielder **Fernandinho (25)** didn't have to cover large distances to his left or right in order to receive from the centre backs.

Fernandinho (25) not only used less energy during the attacking phase, but he also stayed in a central position which enabled him to create an effective double triangle shape with the attacking midfielders and the forward (if he was in a deep position).

In this example, the attacking midfielders are **Silva (21)** and **De Bruyne (17)**. The forward is **Agüero (10)**.

If the forward **Agüero (10)** was in a more advanced position, then a diamond shape was created, which was also a very effective shape during Manchester City's attacking phase.

4. Inverted Full Back in a Central Position = 3 Available Forward Passing Options

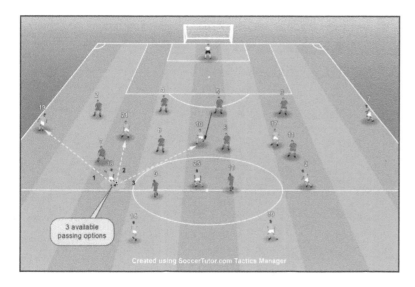

If the full back **Delph (18)** has the ball in a central position, he has 3 forward passing options:

1. Winger **Sané (19)**.
2. Attacking midfielder **Silva (21)**.
3. Forward **Agüero (10)**.

Another important benefit was that the winger was able to receive a pass with a good half-turned body shape, enabling him to move forward immediately after receiving the ball.

5. Full Back in a Wide Position = Only 2 Available Forward Passing Options

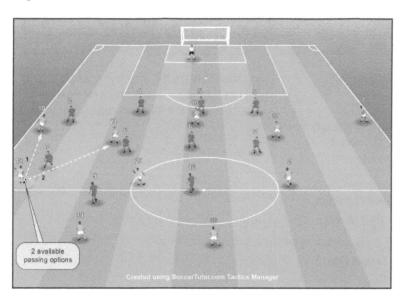

If the full back **Delph (18)** has the ball in a conventional wide position, he only has 2 forward passing options:

1. Winger **Sané (19)**.
2. Attacking midfielder **Silva (21)**.

Also, if the winger receives a pass from a wide positioned full back, he most likely has to receive with his back to goal and there is no way of moving forward immediately.

PEP GUARDIOLA'S ATTACKING TACTICS

ROTATING POSITIONS OF THE INVERTED FULL BACK, ATT. MIDFIELDER AND WINGER TO RETAIN BALANCE

Created using SoccerTutor.com Tactics Manager

In the attacking phase, Pep Guardiola's Manchester City showed fluidity in the positioning of the full back, the winger and the attacking midfielder, but always maintained their balance as a priority. In this way, the benefits of the appropriate positioning were retained.

When the attacking midfielder dropped into a deeper position to receive, as shown by **Silva (21)** in the diagram example, a rotation was carried out.

The full back on the strong side **Delph (18)** moves into a wide position and the winger **Sané (19)** converges towards the centre to provide a passing option, in case the attacking midfielder **Silva (21)** receives from **Laporte (14)**.

Using this rotation, the effective triangle shape and all its important benefits are retained, which will be shown in the following parts of this book.

Positioning and Rotations with Inverted Full Backs

Practice 1: Rotating Movements with Inverted Full Backs in a Passing Rotation Practice

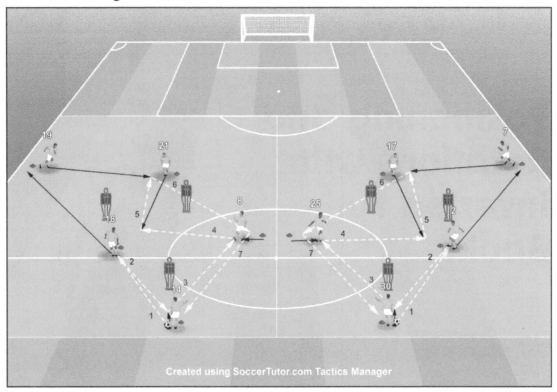

Created using SoccerTutor.com Tactics Manager

Description

There are 2 groups of 5 players who all start positioned on the blue cones. The 2 groups work simultaneously.

The centre back **(14/30)** starts the practice by playing a 1-2 combination with the inverted full back **(18/2)**.

Rotation: As soon as the return pass is made, the attacking midfielder **(21/17)** starts to drop back. This action is the trigger for the players to start the rotation, as the full back **(18/2)** moves wide and the winger **(19/7)** shifts inside.

At the same time, the centre back **(14/30)** passes to the defensive midfielder **(8/25)**, who plays a

first time pass inside to the attacking midfielder **(21/17)** who has dropped back.

The attacking midfielder **(21/17)** receives and passes forward to the winger **(19/7)**, who plays a first time pass back to the defensive midfielder **(8/25)** - he then directs the ball back to the centre back **(14/30)** in the starting position.

The practice continues with the 3 rotating players in new positions.

Coaching Points

1. The attacking midfielder triggers the rotation.

2. Well-timed synchronised movements.

3. High speed passing (1 or 2 touches).

PROGRESSION

Practice 2: Rotating Movements with Inverted Full Backs in 2 Simultaneous Dynamic Games

Created using SoccerTutor.com Tactics Manager

Objective: Attacking after rotating movements in wide areas with inverted full backs.

Description

The marked out area is divided vertically into 2 equal halves and both sides play their games at the same time (simultaneously).

The practice starts with blue the centre back's **(14/30)** pass to one of the defensive midfielders **(8/25)**. As soon as the pass is made, the 3 wide blue players **(18/2 - inverted full back, 21/17 - attacking midfielder & 19/7 - winger)** rotate their positions.

The trigger for the rotation is the dropping back movement of the attacking midfielder **(21/17)**. With this rotation, the blues try to unbalance the opponents and score a goal.

They have a 5 v 4 numerical advantage as the defensive midfielder **(8/25)** enters the playing area.

The blues must score in a limited amount of time (e.g. 15 seconds). If they don't, the coach passes to a red player and the reds try to score as quickly as possible in the mini goal.

The reds defend their goal, try to win the ball and then must score within a limited amount of time (e.g. 8 – 12 seconds) in the mini goal.

Coaching Points

1. Play at a high tempo.
2. There needs to be perfect synchronisation in the 3 players' rotating movements.
3. Quick/accurate finishing (2 touch maximum).

TACTICAL SITUATION 3

Creating and Exploiting Overloads in Wide Areas

Content from Analysis of Manchester City during the 2017/2018 and 2018/2019 Premier League winning seasons

The analysis is based on recurring patterns of play observed within the Manchester City team. Once the same phase of play occurred a number of times (at least 10) the tactics would be seen as a pattern. The analysis on the next page is an example of the team's tactics being used effectively, taken from a specific game.

Each action, pass, individual movement with or without the ball, and the positioning of each player on the pitch including their body shape, are presented.

The analysis is then used to create a full progressive session to coach this specific tactical situation.

CREATING AND EXPLOITING OVERLOADS IN WIDE AREAS

Creating Overloads Out Wide with the Advanced Positioning of the Attacking Midfielders

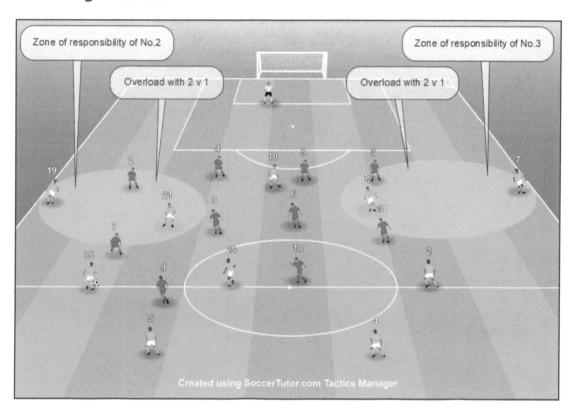

The Manchester City attacking midfielders use intelligent positioning in order to create problems for their opponents.

In the diagram example, we have **Silva (21)** and **De Bruyne (17)** as the attacking midfielders. Pep Guardiola would often use **Gündoğan (8)** and **Bernardo (20)** in these positions also.

The Manchester City attacking midfielders **(21/17)** are both positioned within the zone of responsibility of the respective opposing full back (red No.2/No.3).

This creates a 2v1 overload with the City attacking midfielder **(21/17)** and the winger **(19/7)** against the opposing full back out wide.

EXPLOITING THE OVERLOAD IN A WIDE AREA TO RECEIVE BETWEEN THE LINES AND TURN

1. Attacking Midfielder Receives in Between the Lines when the Opposing Full Back Stays Back to Control the Winger

Controls No. 19

Created using SoccerTutor.com Tactics Manager

After creating a 2v1 overload in a wide area (see diagram on previous page), Manchester City's aim was to exploit this favourable situation and break through the opposition's defence.

The appropriate response in each specific situation depends on the reaction of the opposing full back (red No.2 in diagram).

In this tactical example, the ball is with the inverted full back **Zinchenko (35)**.

The attacking midfielder **Silva (21)** moves towards an available passing lane within the

zone of responsibility of the opposing right back (red No2).

If the pass is directed to the attacking midfielder **Silva (21)**, the next move depends on how the red No.2 reacts.

If red No.2 stays in a deep position to control Man City's left winger **Sané (19)**, the attacking midfielder **Silva (21)** can receive free of marking and turn towards goal - this is shown in the diagram example.

2. Early Cross into the Space Between the Defenders and the GK

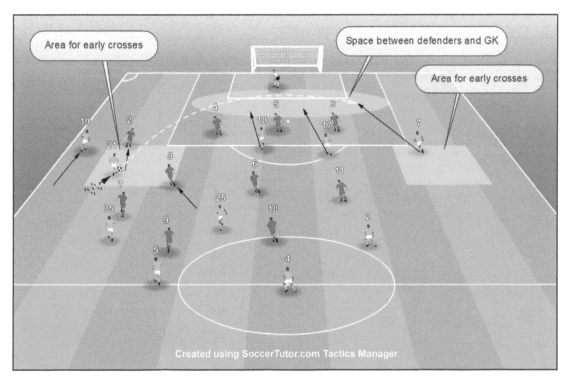

The opposing full back (red No.2) has decided to stay with the winger **Sané (19)** and a 2v1 situation is created in a wide area - see diagram on the previous page.

If red No.2 drops back to control the forward movement of the winger **Sané (19)**, the attacking midfielder in possession **Silva (21)** finds available space to move forward, get close to the penalty area and deliver an early cross.

These kinds of crosses were delivered within the yellow highlighted area to the forward **(10)**, the other attacking midfielder **(17)** or the winger **(7)** - this will be analysed later in the book.

If there was space between the opposing defenders and the goalkeeper, the early cross was directed there to make it difficult for the defenders who are moving back facing their goal.

NOTE:

Manchester City mainly used these crosses when the opposition defended well by retaining good compactness in the defensive line using 5 or even 6 players, and there were limited openings for Guardiola's side to break through them.

The early crosses were delivered by the attacking midfielders, the full backs, or even the wingers when there was a rotation between the 3 - see "Tactical Situation 2: "Positioning and Rotations with Inverted Full Backs."

PEP GUARDIOLA'S ATTACKING TACTICS

3. Winger Stays Free of Marking and Receives High Up the Flank when the Opposing Full Back Closes Down the Winger

This is a variation of the tactical example on the previous page where the opposing full back (red No.2) drops back to track the City left winger **Sané's (19)** run.

In this example, red No.2 instead decides to move forward and contest the attacking midfielder **Silva (21)** on the ball.

As red No.2 closes down **Silva (21)**, the left winger **Sané (19)** is left completely free of marking high up the flank.

Silva (21) plays a simple pass to **Sané (19)**, who receives in a favourable situation to cross into the penalty area for oncoming team-mates.

EXPLOITING THE OVERLOAD BY RECEIVING, TURNING AND MOVING INSIDE WITH THE BALL

1. Receiving Between the Lines via a Sideways Pass to a Link Player (Defensive Midfielder)

Controls No.19

Created using SoccerTutor.com Tactics Manager

If the attacking midfielder **Silva (21)** didn't receive a direct pass from the full back **Zinchenko (35)**, the ball was moved to the attacking midfielder via a link player.

A very effective option was moving the ball to the defensive midfielder **Fernandinho (25)**, who would act as the link player to pass the ball to the attacking midfielder **Silva (21)** between the lines.

The attacking midfielder receiving between the lines could be **Silva (21)**, **De Bruyne (17)**, **Gündoğan (8)** or **Bernardo (20)**.

As the pass was directed from inside (defensive midfielder) to outside (attacking midfielder), this enables **Silva (21)** to receive with a good open body shape (half-turned) and move inside with the ball immediately - this was not always possible after a direct pass from the full back.

2. Options After Receiving Between the Lines, Turning and Moving Inside with the Ball

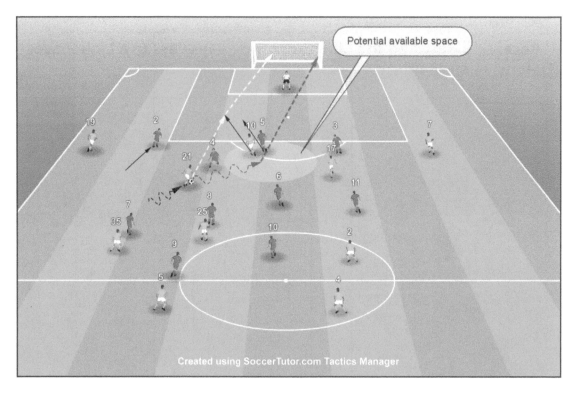

After moving inside with the ball, the attacking midfielder **Silva (21)** is closed down by the opposing centre back (red No.4).

The Manchester City forward **Agüero (10)** sees the red centre back (No.4) leave his position in the defensive line, so he makes a diagonal movement to receive a pass in behind and in the penalty area.

The best option for the attacking midfielder in possession **(Silva - 21 in diagram example)** was the final pass to the forward **Agüero (10)**, who makes a driving run into the available space created in behind the centre back, receives and shoots at goal.

The attacking midfielder would also have the option of other final passes (in behind) to the

other forward moving players, if the situation was favourable with a clear passing lane to them.

The attacking midfielder playing the final pass in behind could be **Silva (21)**, **De Bruyne (17)**, **Gündoğan (8)** or **Bernardo (20)**.

A final option is to utilise the forward **Agüero's (10)** run to dribble into the created space in the centre and shoot at goal - see blue lines in diagram.

MOVING THE BALL TO THE FREE WINGER WHEN PUT UNDER PRESSURE RECEIVING BETWEEN THE LINES

1. Attacking Midfielder's First Time Pass to the Free Winger when Under Pressure from the Opposing Full Back

If the opposing full back (red No.2) moves forward to close down the attacking midfielder **(Silva - 21 in diagram example)** as soon as the pass was played to prevent him from turning, the Manchester City winger **(Sané - 19 in diagram example)** stays free of marking.

In this tactical situation, the aim for the City attacking midfielder was to move the ball to his free team-mate (winger). This was achieved either by a direct pass (as shown in the diagram above) or through combination play (see next page).

In this first example, the quality of **Silva (21)** or **De Bruyne (17)** enables them to read the situation very quickly and make the best decision in a split second.

If there was a possibility to move the ball directly to the winger, the attacking midfielder carried out this action. In the diagram example, **Silva (21)** plays a first time pass to the left winger **Sané (19)**, who is free in space to receive and then dribble forward.

2. Attacking Midfielder Passes Back for Team-mate to Play an Aerial Pass to the Free Winger

In this second example, the opposing full back (red No.2) is able to block the direct pass to **Sané (19)**.

Pep Guardiola's players find other alternatives to direct the ball to the winger, with good combination play.

One option was the back pass, followed by a forward pass played either by the full back **Zinchenko (35)** or the defensive midfielder **Fernandinho (25)**.

3. Attacking Midfielder Passes Inside for Forward to Play a Diagonal Pass to the Free Winger

Another option when the direct pass to the winger was blocked off was the square (inside) pass, followed by a forward pass.

The link player could be the other attacking midfielder **De Bruyne (17)** if he was positioned close to the strong side.

Otherwise it was the forward **Agüero (10)**, as shown in the diagram example. **Agüero (10)** drops back to receive the square inside pass from **Silva (21)** and passes out wide to **Sané (19)**.

EXPLOITING GAPS BETWEEN DEFENDERS

1. Gap Between the Opposing Centre Back and Full Back

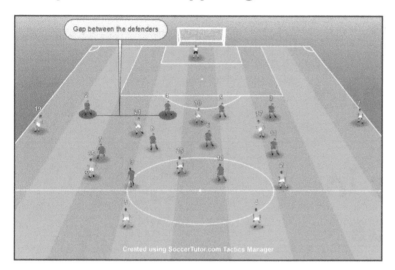

Gap between the defenders

If the opposing full back (red No.2) and centre back (No.4) are not compact and too far apart, a gap is created.

In contrast to the previous examples, the Manchester City attacking midfielder would not drop back to receive between the lines in this situation.

The aim would change to exploiting the gap and receiving in an advanced position.

2. Attacking Midfielder Exploits Gap to Receive in Behind and Cross

In this example, the attacking midfielder **Silva (21)** makes a forward run into the available space between the opposing full back (red No.2) and centre back (No.4).

Silva (21) receives the full back **Zinchenko's (35)** forward pass and is in a good position to deliver a low cross for a team-mate to score.

NOTE:
This attacking move was mainly used after a switch of play, when the opposing centre back didn't manage to shift across in time.

47

SESSION 3 BASED ON THE TACTICS OF **PEP GUARDIOLA**

Creating and Exploiting Overloads in Wide Areas

Practice 1: Exploiting Overloads in Wide Areas by Receiving and Turning to Outside (Pattern)

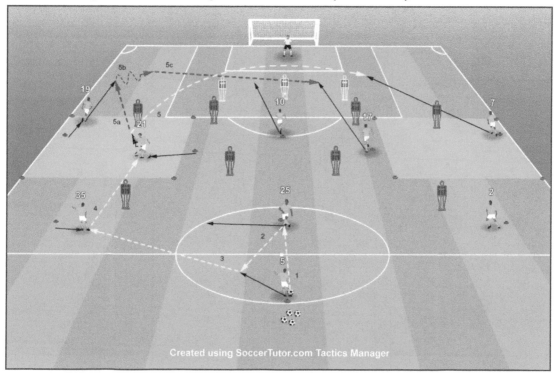

Created using SoccerTutor.com Tactics Manager

Objective: Exploiting overloads (2v1) in wide areas by receiving and turning.

Description

The players start on the blue cones. The 8 red mannequins represent the opponents in formation and the 3 yellow mannequins represent the positioning of the opposing defenders in case of an early cross.

The blues use a specific passing pattern. As soon as the full back **(35)** receives, the defensive midfielder **(25)** offers a passing option inside and the attacking midfielder **(21)** enters the yellow zone to provide a passing option within it.

The ball is passed to the attacking midfielder **(21)**, who turns and then has to decide between

delivering an early cross (5) or passing to the winger (5a) to dribble the ball forward and cross.

The other players **(10, 17 & 7)** use well timed runs into the gaps between the yellow mannequins and try to score.

The practice restarts with the pattern carried out on the right side. There can be 2 players in each position for the 5 advanced players to keep the practice running at a high tempo.

Coaching Points

1. Quality high speed passing (1 or 2 touches).

2. Quality early or high crosses and accurate finishing.

3. Well synchronised movements of the players.

Practice 2: Exploiting Overloads in Wide Areas by Receiving and Turning to Inside (Pattern)

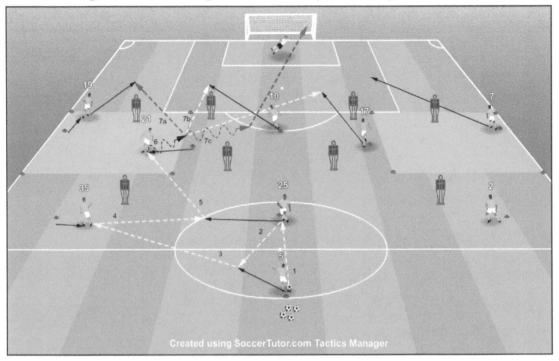

Created using SoccerTutor.com Tactics Manager

Objective: Exploiting overloads (2v1) in wide areas by receiving and turning.

Description

This is a variation of the previous practice pattern.

This time, the pass from the full back **(35)** is directed inside to the defensive midfielder **(25)**, who is used as a link player - the ball is then played to the attacking midfielder **(21)** in the yellow zone, which enables him to receive and turn towards the inside.

As soon as the attacking midfielder **(21)** turns, he dribbles the ball towards the red mannequin (opposing centre back), while his team-mates **(10, 17 & 7)** make well-timed runs in behind to offer multiple final pass options.

The practice restarts with the pattern carried out on the right side.

There can be 2 players in each position for the 5 advanced players to keep the practice running at a high tempo.

Coaching Points

1. Quality high speed passing (1 or 2 touches).
2. Quality low crossing and accurate finishing.
3. Well synchronised movements of the players.

PROGRESSION
Practice 3: Exploiting Overloads in Wide Areas by Moving the Ball to the Free Winger
Scenario A: Full Back Passes to Link Player (Defensive Midfielder)

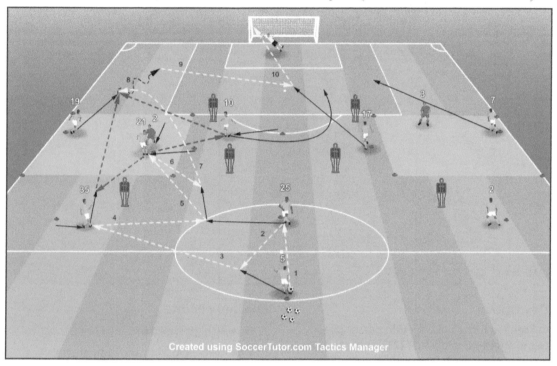

Created using SoccerTutor.com Tactics Manager

Objective: Exploiting overloads (2v1) in wide areas by moving the ball to the free winger.

Description (Scenario A)

This is a progression of the previous practice. We add 2 red full backs inside the wide <u>yellow zones</u>, who are coached to press the blue attacking midfielders as soon as the pass is played to them.

IN Scenario A, the initial passing pattern has the defensive midfielder **(25)** passing to the attacking midfielder **(21)** after an inside pass from the full back **(35)**.

As soon as the pass to the attacking midfielder **(21)** is played, the opposing full back (red No.2) moves forward to press him.

There are 3 options:

1. Pass back to the defensive midfielder **(25)**, who plays an aerial pass to the free winger **(19)** - see yellow arrows.

2. Pass back to the full back **(35)**, who passes to the free winger **(19)** - see red arrows.

3. Inside pass to the forward **(10)**, who then passes to the winger **(19)** - see blue arrows.

The advanced team-mates **(10, 17 & 7)** make well-timed runs into the penalty area to receive the cross and finish on goal.

The practice restarts with the pattern carried out on the right side.

Scenario B: Full Back Passes Direct to the Attacking Midfielder

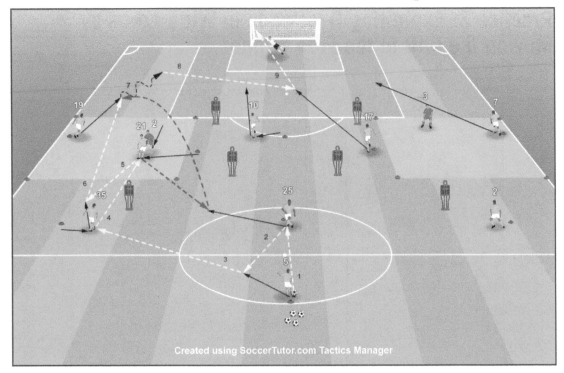

Created using SoccerTutor.com Tactics Manager

Description (Scenario B)

In Scenario B, the full back **(35)** passes directly to the attacking midfielder **(21)**, so there is no inside pass to the defensive midfielder **(25)**.

From this point, the practice is exactly the same as Scenario A (see previous page), except the third option of the inside pass to the forward is not possible.

The practice restarts with the pattern carried out on the right side.

There can be 2 players in each position for the 5 advanced players to keep the practice running at a high tempo.

Coaching Points

1. Quality high speed passing (1 or 2 touches).
2. Quality low crossing and accurate finishing.
3. Well synchronised movements of the players.

Practice 4: Reading the Opponent's Reactions to Best Exploit Overloads in Wide Areas

Scenario A: Opposing Full Back Stays Back to Control the Winger

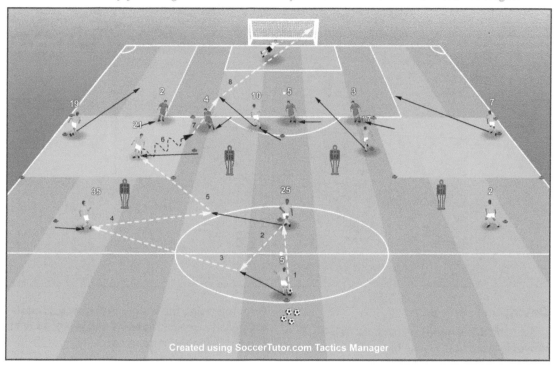

Created using SoccerTutor.com Tactics Manager

Objective: Exploiting the overload wide in different ways, depending on the reactions and movements of opposing defenders.

Description (Scenario A)

This is a progression of the previous practice with the blues now playing against 4 active red defenders.

The red full backs within the yellow zones decide whether to move forward and press the blue attacking midfielder or not.

The blue players have to read the reaction of the red full back (No.2 in diagram example) and best exploit the overload by using the right decision making.

In Scenario A, the red full back (No.2) decides to stay back and control the blue winger **(19)** instead of moving forward to pressure the attacking midfielder **(21)**.

This means the attacking midfielder **(21)** is able to receive inside the yellow zone, turn and play a final pass in behind.

In the diagram example, **No.21** dribbles inside and plays a simple final pass into the penalty area to the forward **(10)**, who tries to score.

Scenario B: Opposing Full Back Moves to Press Attacking Midfielder

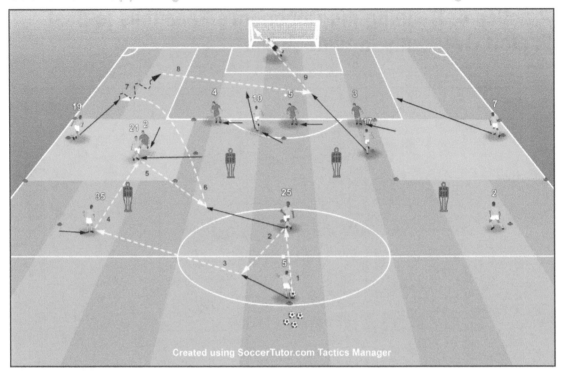

Created using SoccerTutor.com Tactics Manager

Description (Scenario B)

In Scenario B, the opposing full back (red No.2) moves forward to press the blue attacking midfielder **(21)** within the <u>yellow zone</u> and prevents him from turning.

This time, the ball is moved to the free winger **(19)** after a passing combination.

There are 3 options:

1. Pass back to the defensive midfielder **(25)**, who plays an aerial pass to the free winger **(19)** - see diagram example above.

2. Pass back to the full back **(35)**, who passes to the free winger **(19)** - see Page 51.

3. Inside pass to the forward **(10)**, who then passes to the winger **(19)** - see Page 51.

From this point, the winger **(19)** can cross into the penalty area for his team-mates **(10, 17 & 7)**. The red defenders defend normally.

The practice restarts on the right side.

Coaching Points

1. Read the tactical situation i.e. the attacking midfielder **(21 or 17)** should be aware of the reaction of the opposing full back.

2. Quality high speed passing (1 or 2 touches).

3. Quality low crossing and accurate finishing.

4. Well synchronised movements of the players.

PROGRESSION

Practice 5: Exploiting 2v1 Overloads Out Wide in a Dynamic Small Sided Game

Created using SoccerTutor.com Tactics Manager

Objective: Exploiting the overload wide in different ways, depending on the reactions and movements of opposing defenders.

Description

This is a progression of the previous practice, moving into a 9 v 8 (+GK) game. The blue team start the game with the centre back's **(5)** pass from the end line.

The blue team can score in any way (1 point), but if they score after exploiting a 2v1 overload out wide, they score 2 points.

Please see all analysis and practices in this section for different ways the blues can combine and score. The decision making is down to the awareness of the attacking midfielder **(21)**, who must choose the right option depending on the reaction of the opposing full back.

In this example, the red full back (No.2) stays back to control the blue winger **(19)**, so the blue attacking midfielder **(21)** receives between the lines, turns and delivers an early cross into the space between the defenders and the GK.

If the reds win possession, they try to score in either mini goal within 10-12 seconds (2 points).

Coaching Points

1. Read the tactical situation i.e. the attacking midfielder **(21 or 17)** should be aware of the reaction of the opposing full back.

2. Well synchronised movements of the players.

PROGRESSION

Practice 6: Exploiting 2v1 Overloads Out Wide in a Conditioned Game

Created using SoccerTutor.com Tactics Manager

Objective: Exploiting the overload wide in different ways, depending on the reactions and movements of opposing defenders.

Description

In this final practice of the session, the 2 teams play a conditioned 11v11 game. The practice starts from the blue team's goalkeeper.

The blue team can score in any way (1 point), but if they score after exploiting a 2v1 overload out wide, they score 2 points.

Please see all analysis and practices in this section for different ways the blues can combine and score.

If the reds win possession, they try to score within 12-15 seconds (2 points).

Coaching Points

1. Read the tactical situation i.e. the attacking midfielder **(21 or 17)** should be aware of the reaction of the opposing full back.

2. Well synchronised movements of the players.

TACTICAL SITUATION 4

Attacking Options when the Overload Out Wide is Blocked

Content from Analysis of Manchester City during the 2017/2018 and 2018/2019 Premier League winning seasons

The analysis is based on recurring patterns of play observed within the Manchester City team. Once the same phase of play occurred a number of times (at least 10) the tactics would be seen as a pattern. The analysis on the next page is an example of the team's tactics being used effectively, taken from a specific game.

Each action, pass, individual movement with or without the ball, and the positioning of each player on the pitch including their body shape, are presented.

The analysis is then used to create a full progressive session to coach this specific tactical situation.

ATTACKING OPTIONS WHEN THE OVERLOAD OUT WIDE IS BLOCKED

1. The Diagonal Inside Passing Lane is Widened when the Opposition Block the Overload Out Wide

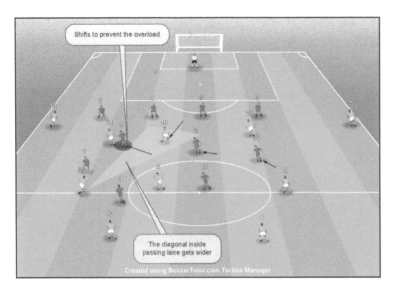

If the opposing central midfielder (8) shifted across extensively to prevent the overload and the other central midfielder (6) didn't carry out the same movement, the diagonal inside passing lane widened and the possibilities of moving the ball to the forward **Agüero (10)** in a crucial area increased.

Agüero (10) drops back to receive and then exploit the situation, depending on the reaction of the red centre back (4).

2. Forward Receives in the Available Passing Lane and Turns when the Opposing Centre Back Stays Back

The Manchester City left back **Zinchenko (35)** uses the diagonal inside passing lane to pass to the forward.

Agüero (10) is able to receive and turn because the red centre back (No.4) decides to defend the space, rather than move forward to press the ball.

Agüero (10) has at least 3 available passing options in behind, as shown in the diagram with **19, 21 & 20**.

3. Forward is Prevented from Turning by the Opposing Centre Back

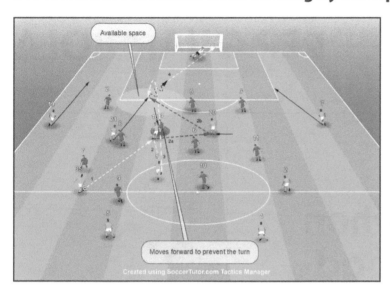

This is a variation of the previous tactical example.

If the red centre back (No.4) moves to press the forward **Agüero (10)**, he cannot turn but there is available space created in behind.

This space is exploited by the attacking midfielder **Silva (21)** after a passing combination similar to those shown earlier in the book, with a back pass to the defensive midfielder **Gündoğan (8)**, followed by a forward pass in behind.

4. Switching Play to the Weak Side into Available Space for a 2v1 Overload Out Wide

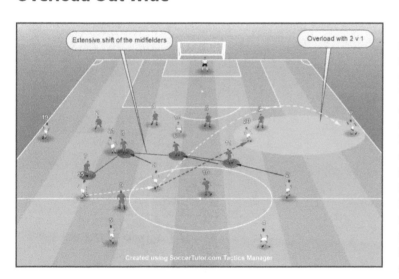

If there was an extensive shift from all the opposing midfielders and the through passing lanes were narrow, there would then be available space and a probable overload on the weak side. Pep Guardiola's Manchester City team react to this tactical situation by switching play to the weak side. In this example, the defensive midfielder **Gündoğan (8)** plays a long pass to the right winger **Sterling (7)** and there is a 2v1 overload.

NOTE:

This tactical situation will be more thoroughly analysed in a later section of this book: "Tactical Situation 11: Switching Play to the Weak Side when the Overload is Blocked Against the 4-3-3."

Attacking Options when the Overload Out Wide is Blocked

Practice 1: Attacking Options when the Overload Out Wide is Blocked in a Functional Practice (vs 4 Players)

Scenario A: 1 Opposing Central Midfielder Shifts Across

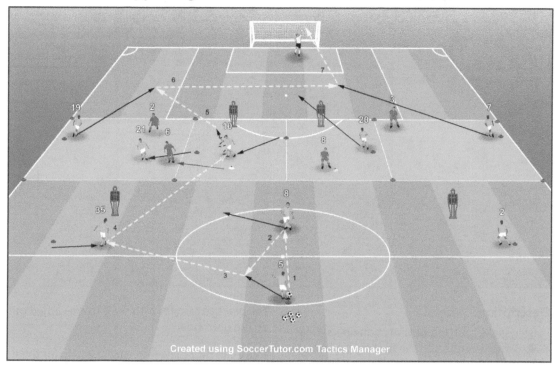

Created using SoccerTutor.com Tactics Manager

Description (Scenario A)

This practice is designed in the same way as the session in "Tactical Situation 3: Creating and Exploiting Overloads in Wide Areas."

Now there are 2 central white zones with 2 red central midfielders (No.6 & No.8). There are also 2 red full backs (No.2 & No.3) in the wide yellow zones. The blue players start on the blue cones and they use a specific passing pattern.

As soon as the full back **(35)** receives, the defensive midfielder **(8)** offers a passing option inside and the attacking midfielder **(21)** enters the yellow zone to try and create a 2v1 overload in a wide area.

If the red central midfielder (8) doesn't enter the yellow zone, then the blue players try to exploit the 2v1 overload, as in the previous section.

If the red central midfielder (6) moves across into the yellow zone, the 2v1 overload out wide isn't possible and the blue forward **(10)** makes a dropping back movement.

The diagonal inside passing lane is widened and the full back **(35)** passes to the forward **(10)** in the white zone.

The forward **(10)** is able to receive in the available space, turn and play a pass in behind (to No.19 in diagram example).

Scenario B: 2 Opposing Central Midfielders Shift Across

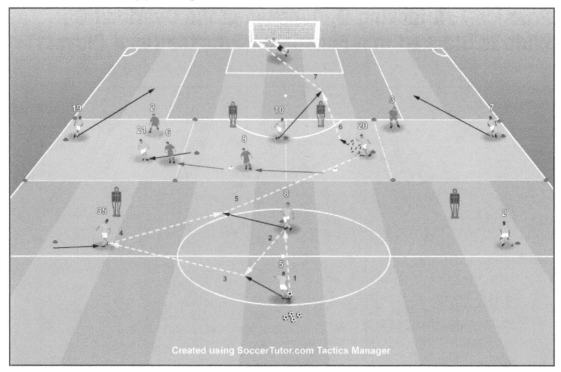

Created using SoccerTutor.com Tactics Manager

Description (Scenario B)

In Scenario B, both red central midfielders (No.6 & No.8) move across and the passing lanes towards the blue attacking midfielder **(21)** and the forward **(10)** are blocked.

In this situation (Scenario B), the full back **(35)** passes inside to the defensive midfielder **(8)** and he is used to move the ball to the other side.

There is available space and a probable overload on the weak side. In this example, the defensive midfielder **(8)** passes to the attacking midfielder **(20)**, but he could also play a long pass (switch play) to the winger **(7)** in the yellow zone for a 2v1 overload out wide.

The attacking midfielder **(20)** receives within the white zone in the available space and is able to turn and play a pass in behind (to No.10 in diagram).

The practice restarts with the pattern carried out on the right side.

There can be 2 players in each position for the 5 advanced players to keep the practice running at a high tempo.

Coaching Points

1. The forward **(10)** and the full back **(35)** need to be able to concentrate and read the tactical situation i.e. whether 1 or 2 red central midfielders shift across.

2. Quality high speed passing (1 or 2 touches).

3. Quality low crossing and accurate finishing.

4. Well synchronised movements of the players.

PROGRESSION

Practice 2: Attacking Options when the Overload Out Wide is Blocked in a Functional Practice (vs 6 Players)

Scenario A: Forward Receives in Space and Turns

Created using SoccerTutor.com Tactics Manager

Description (Scenario A)

This is a progression of the previous practice and 2 active red centre backs (4 & 5) are added. After moving the ball to the full back **(35)**, the blues now have to read the tactical situation and make the right decisions about where to direct the ball to exploit the specific tactical situation.

The red central midfielder (No.6) moves across into the wide yellow zone, so the blue forward **(10)** drops back and the diagonal inside passing lane is widened. The full back **(35)** passes to the forward **(10)** in the central white zone.

Whether or not the forward **(10)** can turn depends on the reaction of the red centre back (No.4) - see Scenario B on next page.

In this example (Scenario A), the red centre back (No.4) stays back and does not move to press the forward **(10)**, so he is able to receive within the white zone, turn and play a pass in behind (to the winger No.19 in diagram).

The practice restarts with the pattern carried out on the right side.

NOTE: If the other red central midfielder (No.8) makes an extensive shift across and the passing lane towards the blue forward **(10)** is blocked, the full back **(35)** will instead pass inside to the defensive midfielder **(8)** - see Scenario C.

Scenario B: Forward is Prevented from Turning

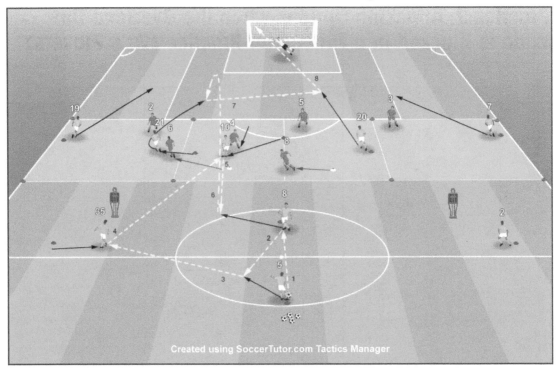

Created using SoccerTutor.com Tactics Manager

Description (Scenario B)

In Scenario B, the opposing centre back (red No.4) moves forward to press the blue forward **(10)** and prevents him from turning within the central <u>white zone</u>.

The forward's **(10)** aim is now to move the ball to a team-mate, so they can direct the ball into the available space in behind red No.4.

The forward **(10)** passes the ball back to the defensive midfielder **(8)**, who plays an aerial pass in behind to the attacking midfielder **(21)**.

The attacking midfielder **(21)** can try to score or pass to team-mate to score (to the attacking midfielder No.20 in diagram example).

The practice restarts with the pattern carried out on the right side.

Scenario C: Passing Lane to the Forward is Blocked

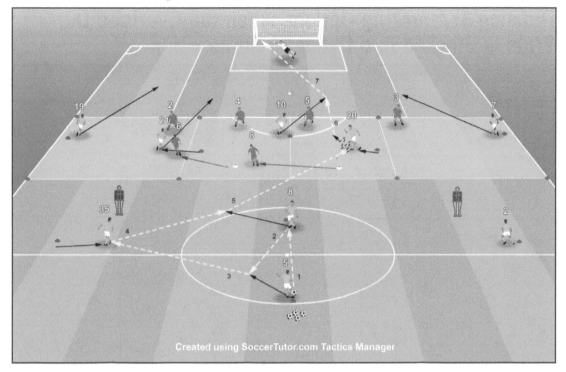

Created using SoccerTutor.com Tactics Manager

Description (Scenario C)

In Scenario C, the second red central midfielder (No.8) makes an extensive shift across and the passing lane towards the blue forward (10) is blocked, so he does not drop back.

The full back (35) passes inside to the defensive midfielder (8) and he is used to move the ball to the weak side, where there is available space and a probable overload.

In this example, the defensive midfielder (8) passes to the attacking midfielder (20) within the central white zone, but he could also play a long pass (switch play) to the winger (7) for a 2v1 overload out wide in the yellow zone.

The attacking midfielder (20) receives in the available space and is able to turn and play a pass in behind (to No.10 in diagram).

The practice restarts with the pattern carried out on the right side.

Coaching Points

1. The forward (10) and the full back (35) need to be able to concentrate and read the reactions of the opposing central midfielders and centre backs.

2. Quality high speed passing (1 or 2 touches).

3. Quality low crossing and accurate finishing.

4. Well synchronised movements of the players.

PROGRESSION

Practice 3: Attacking Options when the Overload Out Wide is Blocked in a Dynamic Game

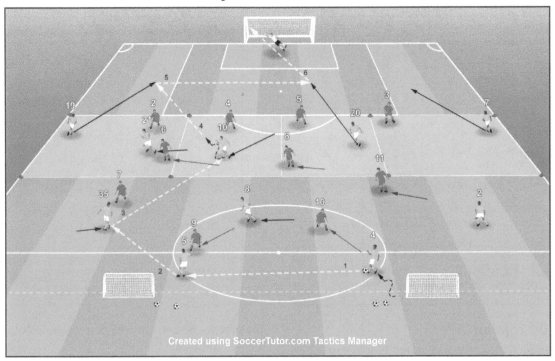

Created using SoccerTutor.com Tactics Manager

Description

This is a progression of the previous practice, moving into a 10 v 10 (+GK) game.

The blue team can score in any way (1 point), but if they score after exploiting a 2v1 overload out wide or successfully use one of the attacking options displayed in the previous practices successfully when the overload is blocked, they score 2 points.

In this example, the red central midfielder (No.6) moves across into the <u>yellow zone</u>, so the blue forward **(10)** drops back and the diagonal inside passing lane is widened. The full back **(35)** passes to the forward **(10)** in the central <u>white zone</u>.

The red centre back (No.4) stays back and does not move to press the blue forward **(10)**, so he is

able to receive within the <u>white zone</u>, turn and play a pass in behind (to No.19 in diagram).

The reds try to win the ball and then score in either mini goal within 8 – 12 seconds (2 points).

Coaching Points

1. The forward **(10)** and the full back **(35)** need to concentrate and read the reactions of the opposing central midfielders and centre backs.

2. Quality high speed passing (1 or 2 touches).

3. Quality low crossing and accurate finishing.

4. Well synchronised movements of the players.

PROGRESSION

Practice 4: Attacking Options when the Overload Out Wide is Blocked in a Conditioned Game

Created using SoccerTutor.com Tactics Manager

Description

In this final practice of the session, the 2 teams play a conditioned 11v11 game. The practice starts from the blue team's goalkeeper.

The blue team can score in any way (1 point), but if they score after exploiting a 2v1 overload out wide or successfully use one of the attacking options displayed in the previous practices successfully when the overload is blocked, they score 2 points.

Please see the tactical analysis and all practices in this session for different ways the blues can combine and score.

In this example, both red central midfielders (No.6 & No.8) have shifted across, so the passing lane to the blue forward **(10)** is blocked.

Therefore, the left back **(35)** passes inside to the defensive midfielder **(8)** and he moves the ball to the attacking midfielder on the weak side **(20)**, who is in space to receive.

If the reds win possession, they try to score within 12-15 seconds (2 points).

TACTICAL SITUATION 5

Moving the Ball Wide and Receiving in Behind the Full Back (or Create Space for Inside Pass)

Content from Analysis of Manchester City during the 2017/2018 and 2018/2019 Premier League winning seasons

The analysis is based on recurring patterns of play observed within the Manchester City team. Once the same phase of play occurred a number of times (at least 10) the tactics would be seen as a pattern. The analysis on the next page is an example of the team's tactics being used effectively, taken from a specific game.

Each action, pass, individual movement with or without the ball, and the positioning of each player on the pitch including their body shape, are presented.

The analysis is then used to create a full progressive session to coach this specific tactical situation.

PEP GUARDIOLA'S ATTACKING TACTICS

MOVING THE BALL WIDE AND RECEIVING IN BEHIND THE FULL BACK

1. Opposing Full Back's Wide Position Restricts Space for Winger

When the Manchester City full backs want to play to the winger, the options used depend on the opposing full back's positioning.

If the opposing full back takes up a wide position to restrict the space for the City winger, he is unable to receive the ball to feet, facing the opponent's goal.

2. Long Pass in Behind the Full Back (Through Ball Between FB & CB)

The winger **Sané (19)** does not try to receive to feet in this situation - he exploits the space in behind the full back instead.

The City wingers either drop back to unbalance the opposing full back and then quickly change direction into the space behind the opponent, or use a sudden diagonal movement behind the back of the full back.

NOTE:

Both **Sané (19)** and **Sterling (7)** have the necessary explosiveness and speed to carry out this kind of action, while players like **Zinchenko (35)** and **Delph (18)** on the left and **Walker (2)** or **Danilo (3)** on the right have the technical ability to play through balls.

EXPLOITING THE SPACE BEHIND THE FULL BACK AFTER MOVING THE BALL WIDE

1. Winger Receives in Space Out Wide Facing the Opponent's Goal

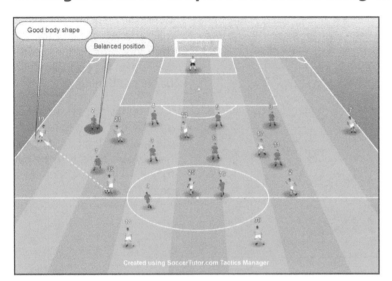

If the opposing full back was in a more balanced position, the through balls were prevented, but the winger had more available space to receive facing the opponent's goal.

The City full back is in a central position (Pep Guardiola's inverted full backs) so there is an angle to the pass, which helps the winger receive with an open body shape.

2. Opposing Full Back Closes Down the Winger and the Attacking Midfielder Runs Forward to Receive in the Space Created Behind

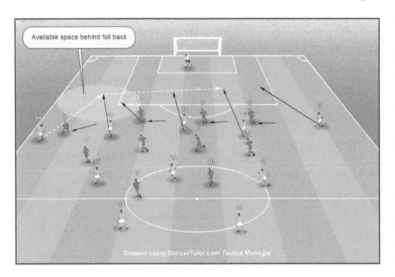

The red right back (No.2) moves to close down **Sané (19)** and as soon as he receives, the attacking midfielder **Silva (21)** makes a run behind the back of red No.2 to receive in the available space and cross into the penalty area.

If red No.4 moves to contest the City attacking midfielder **(Silva - 21 in diagram)**, it was then probable there would be a 3 v 2 numerical advantage for City inside the penalty area.

USING THE RUN BEHIND THE FULL BACK TO CREATE SPACE FOR AN INSIDE PASS TO THE FORWARD

1. Attacking Midfielder Makes a Deep Run to Occupy the Opposing Centre Back and Create Space Between the Lines for the Forward

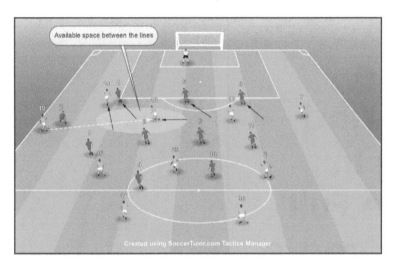

The City attacking midfielder **Silva (21)** makes a forward run and is tracked by the red centre back (No.4). The other red centre back (No.5) and the left back (No.3) drop back to keep the defensive line balanced, which creates space between the lines.

The forward **Agüero (10)** shifts across to receive free of marking. Red No.5 cannot close down **Agüero (10)** because a very large gap would be left in the centre of defence.

2. The Forward Has 3 Available Passing Options in Behind

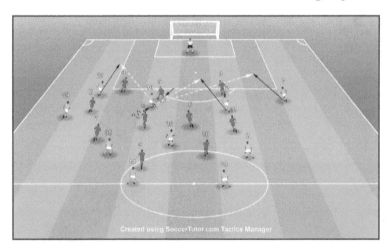

The winger **Sané (19)** has passed inside to the forward **Agüero (10)**, who receives and turns in a crucial area for key passes.

Agüero (10) has 3 passing options in behind.

As the opposing right back (No.2) is in an advanced position and unable to intervene, City have a 4 v 3 numerical advantage near the opposition's penalty area.

PEP GUARDIOLA'S ATTACKING TACTICS

Moving the Ball Wide and Receiving in Behind the Full Back (or Create Space for Inside Pass)

Practice 1: Receive in Behind the Full Back or Create Space for Inside Pass in a Functional Practice

Scenario A: Opposing Centre Back Stays in Position

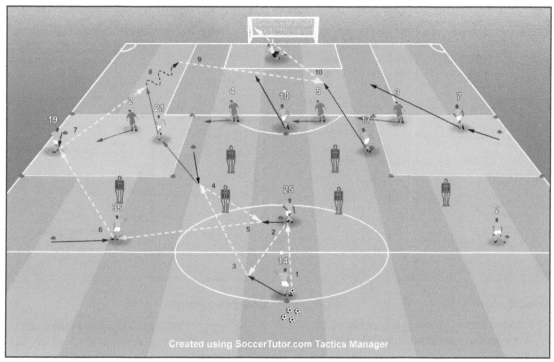

Created using SoccerTutor.com Tactics Manager

Objective: Reading the reactions of the opposing defenders to either pass in behind the full back or pass inside (between the lines).

Description (Scenario A)

The blue players start on the blue cones and they play against a red back 4.

The blues use a specific passing pattern. As soon as the full back **(35)** receives, the attacking midfielder **(21)** makes a run behind the back of the red right back (No.2) and the full back **(35)** passes to the free winger **(19)** in the <u>yellow zone</u>.

The red full back (No.2) is coached to let the winger receive and then move to press him.

The blue winger **(19)** must read the positioning and reaction of the centre back on the strong side (red No.4).

In Scenario A, the red centre back (4) doesn't track the run of the blue attacking midfielder **(21)**, so he is able to receive the pass from the winger in behind red No.2.

The player who receives from the winger (No.21 in this example - Scenario A) should focus on taking the best option when crossing, passing or shooting.

The practice restarts with the pattern carried out on the right side.

Scenario B: Opposing Centre Back Tracks Attacking Midfielder's Run

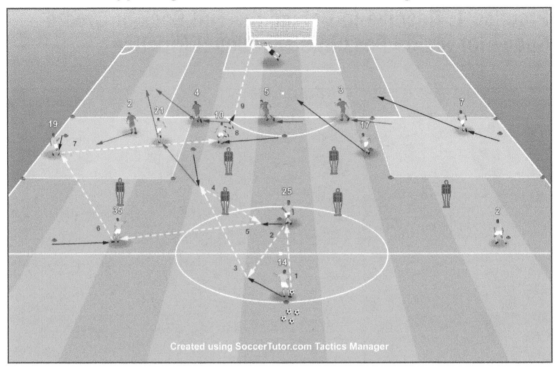

Created using SoccerTutor.com Tactics Manager

Description (Scenario B)

In Scenario B, the opposing centre back (red No.4) tracks the run of the blue attacking midfielder **(21)**.

The blue forward **(10)** reads the situation and moves across. There is space created for an inside pass to the forward **(10)** to receive free of marking.

The forward **(10)** should focus on taking the best option to either pass in behind for a team-mate or shoot, as shown in the diagram example.

The practice restarts with the pattern carried out on the right side.

Coaching Points

1. The winger **(19)** and the forward **(10)** need to concentrate and read the reactions of the opposing centre back.

2. Quality high speed passing (1 or 2 touches).

3. Quality crossing and well-timed final passes.

4. Well synchronised movements of the players (especially the winger and attacking midfielder).

Practice 2: Receive in Behind the Full Back or Create Space for Inside Pass in a Small Sided Game

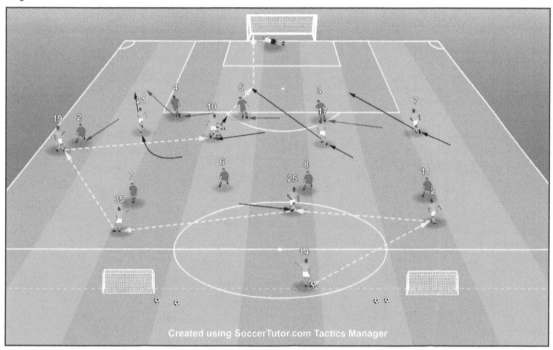

Created using SoccerTutor.com Tactics Manager

Objective: Reading the reactions of the opposing defenders to either pass in behind the full back or pass inside (between the lines).

Description

This is a progression of the previous practice, moving into a 9 v 8 (+GK) game.

The blue team start the practice with the centre back's (14) pass from the end line.

The blue team can score in any way (1 point), but if they score after moving the ball wide to the winger (19 or 7) and pass in behind the full back or play into the forward (10) between the lines, they score 2 points.

Please see the tactical analysis and all practices in this session for different ways the blues can combine and score.

In this example, the red centre back (No.4) tracks the run of the blue attacking midfielder (21). The blue forward (10) reads the situation and moves across.

There is space created for the winger (21) to play an inside pass to the forward (10), who receives free of marking in between the lines.

If the reds win possession, they try to score in either mini goal within 10-12 seconds (2 points).

Coaching Points

1. The winger (19) and the forward (10) need to concentrate and read the reactions of the opposing centre back.

2. Well synchronised movements of the players (especially the winger and attacking midfielder).

PROGRESSION

Practice 3: Receive in Behind the Full Back or Create Space for Inside Pass in a Conditioned Game

Created using SoccerTutor.com Tactics Manager

Description

In this final practice of the session, the 2 teams play a conditioned 11v11 game. The game starts from the blue team's goalkeeper.

The blue team can score in any way (1 point), but if they score after moving the ball wide to the winger **(19 or 7)** and pass in behind the full back or play into the forward **(10)** between the lines, they score 2 points.

Please see the tactical analysis and all practices in this session for different ways the blues can combine and score.

In this example, the red full back (No.3) is in a wide position to restrict the space of the blue winger **(7)**.

The winger **(7)** does not try to receive to feet in this situation - he instead exploits the space in behind red No.3 by first dropping back to unbalance his opponent and then quickly changes direction and receives the through ball from the full back **(2)** in behind.

If the reds win possession, they try to score within 12-15 seconds (2 points).

TACTICAL SITUATION 6

Combination Play Out Wide when the Overload is Blocked

Content from Analysis of Manchester City during the 2017/2018 and 2018/2019 Premier League winning seasons

The analysis is based on recurring patterns of play observed within the Manchester City team. Once the same phase of play occurred a number of times (at least 10) the tactics would be seen as a pattern. The analysis on the next page is an example of the team's tactics being used effectively, taken from a specific game.

Each action, pass, individual movement with or without the ball, and the positioning of each player on the pitch including their body shape, are presented.

The analysis is then used to create a full progressive session to coach this specific tactical situation.

MOVING THE BALL WIDE WHEN THE OVERLOAD IS BLOCKED

1. Moving the Ball Wide when the Overload is Blocked

Created using SoccerTutor.com Tactics Manager

If the opposing central midfielder on the strong side (red No.8 in diagram) shifts close to the Manchester City attacking midfielder **(De Bruyne - 17 in diagram)** and blocks the overload while the full back **(Zinchenko - 35 in diagram)** passed the ball wide to the winger **(Sané - 19 in diagram)**, the options for Pep Guardiola's team are limited because the opposition are well organised.

However, there are still options to break through the opposition's defensive organisation which have been very successful for Manchester City - they are detailed on the following pages of this section.

2. Both the Pass in Behind the Opposing Full Back to the Attacking Midfielder and the Pass Inside to the Forward Are Blocked

Created using SoccerTutor.com Tactics Manager

As soon as the ball is moved to the winger **Sané (19)**, the attacking midfielder **De Bruyne (17)** makes a forward run to receive in behind the opposing full back (red No.2).

However, the red central midfielder (No.8) follows the run and prevents **De Bruyne (17)** from receiving.

As the forward **Agüero (10)** moves towards the strong side to receive, he is marked by the opposing centre back (red No. 4) who moves forward to restrict the space, while the defensive line stays balanced.

The other 2 red defenders (No.5 and No.3) control the space around the penalty area and the chances of Manchester City creating a scoring opportunity are limited.

NOTE:

When the space behind the opposing full back was restricted, Guardiola's Manchester City team would often aim to move the ball to the weak side and try to create a favourable situation there.

However, they can also use quick combination play on the strong side in this situation - see "One-Two Combination" and "Give-and-Go" examples on following pages.

ONE-TWO COMBINATION OUT WIDE WHEN THE OVERLOAD IS BLOCKED

One-Two Combination Between Winger and Attacking Midfielder

Created using SoccerTutor.com Tactics Manager

In situations when the overload is blocked and the ball is moved to the winger, Pep Guardiola's Manchester City team create scoring opportunities by using quick combination play.

Instead of making a forward run in behind the opposing full back (like in the example on the previous page), the attacking midfielder **De Bruyne (17)** makes a dummy movement to get free of marking and then moves across to provide a passing option for City's left winger **Sané (19)**, who is in possession out wide.

Sané (19) dribbles inside and plays a 1-2 combination with the attacking midfielder **De Bruyne (17)**.

The winger **Sané (19)** receives in behind the opposing full back (red No.2) and crosses into the penalty area for oncoming team-mates.

GIVE-AND-GO COMBINATION WHEN THE OVERLOAD IS BLOCKED

1. Moving the Ball Wide to Carry Out a Give-and-Go Combination

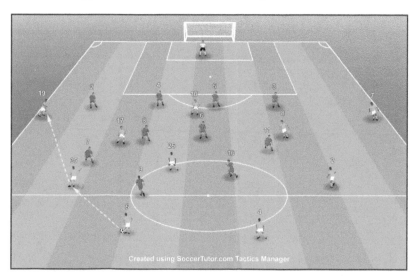

Manchester City frequently use the give-and-go when the overload is blocked - the winger combines with the defensive midfielder, the attacking midfielder or even the full back.

The ball is passed to the winger **Sané (19)** with the opposing central midfielder on the strong side (red No.8) positioned close to City's attacking midfielder **De Bruyne (17)**.

2. Attacking Midfielder Creates Space for the Winger to Pass Back to the Defensive Midfielder

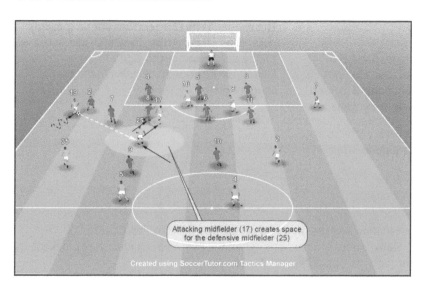

Attacking midfielder (17) creates space for the defensive midfielder (25)

The City winger **Sané (19)** receives, dribbles the ball inside and the attacking midfielder **De Bruyne (17)** moves forward to drag his marker (red No.8) away.

Sané (19) passes diagonally back to the defensive midfielder **Fernandinho (25)**, who has moved into the available space created by **De Bruyne's (17)** forward run.

3. The Winger Makes a Cutting Movement (Inside and then Behind) to Receive Inside the Penalty Area

Created using SoccerTutor.com Tactics Manager

As soon as the pass is played by the winger **Sané (19)**, the red defenders move forward to make their team shape more compact and restrict the space between the lines.

At the same time, the City winger **Sané (19)** moves towards the inside and then changes direction to run forward and in behind (curved movement to avoid being caught offside).

The rather simple movement is very effective at the moment the red defenders are focused on their forward movement, rather than controlling the City players.

The winger **Sané (19)** receives after a through pass (or aerial pass) from the defensive midfielder **Fernandinho (25)**. He is in a favourable position to deliver a low cross or shoot at goal.

NOTE:

Both the 1-2 combination and the give-and-go are also used by Pep Guardiola's Manchester City team in normal situations (when the overload out wide isn't blocked), in order to break through the opposition's defence.

Combination Play Out Wide when the Overload is Blocked

Practice 1: Combination Play Out Wide in a Technical Passing Practice

Scenario A: One-Two Combination with the Attacking Midfielder

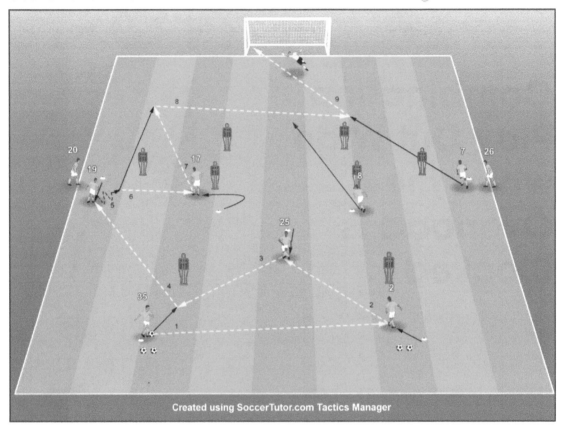

Created using SoccerTutor.com Tactics Manager

Objective: Combination play out wide to break through the opposition's defence.

Description (Scenario A)

In a 35 x 45 yard area, the practice starts with the full back **(No.35 in diagram)**.

The blues use a specific passing pattern. As soon as the winger **(19)** receives from the full back **(35)**, he either dribbles the ball towards the mannequin or towards the inside, depending on the reaction of the attacking midfielder **(17)**.

In Scenario A, the attacking midfielder **(17)** makes a dummy movement (checks away) to get free of marking and moves in front of the mannequin to offer a passing option.

The winger **(19)** passes inside and makes a forward run behind the mannequin to receive the return pass (1-2 combination).

The practice restarts with the pattern carried out on the right side. Have 2 players in the winger positions to keep the practice at a high tempo.

Scenario B: Give-and-Go with the Defensive Midfielder

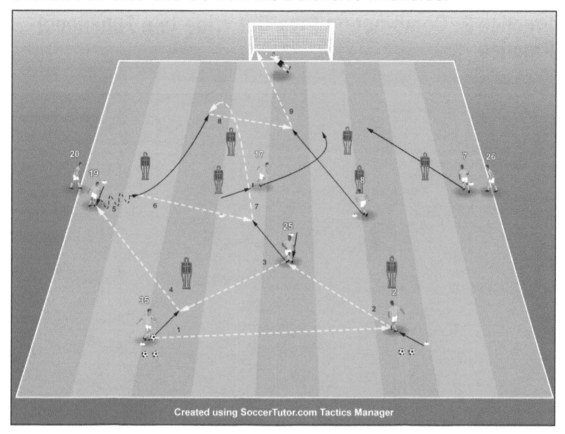

Created using SoccerTutor.com Tactics Manager

Description (Scenario B)

In Scenario B, the attacking midfielder **(17)** moves diagonally forward as soon as the winger **(19)** receives. This movement is made to take away his marker.

The defensive midfielder **(25)** then moves forward in the available space created by the attacking midfielder's **(17)** forward movement. The winger **(19)** passes diagonally back to the defensive midfielder **(25)**.

Immediately after passing back, the winger **(19)** makes a curved run in front of the mannequin (to avoid being in an offside position), receives the aerial pass from the defensive midfielder **(25)** on the run and crosses for his oncoming team-mates **(17, 8 or 7)** to score.

The practice restarts with the pattern carried out on the right side.

Have 2 players in the winger positions to keep the practice at a high tempo.

Coaching Points

1. Quality high speed passing (1 or 2 touches).
2. Well-timed runs by the wingers.
3. Quality low crosses.
4. Well synchronised movements of the players.

PROGRESSION

Practice 2: Combination Play Out Wide in a Functional Practice

Scenario A: One-Two Combination with the Attacking Midfielder

Created using SoccerTutor.com Tactics Manager

Objective: Combination play out wide to break through the opposition's defence (decision making dependant on the attacking midfielder's movement).

Description (Scenario A)

This is a progression of the previous practice and all the blue players start on the blue cones. They play against 2 red central midfielders (No.6 & No.8) and 2 full backs (No.2 & No.3).

The blues use a specific passing pattern. As soon as the winger **(19)** receives, he must read the movement of the attacking midfielder **(17)** to decide whether to use a 1-2 combination with the attacking midfielder **(17)** or a give-and-go with the defensive midfielder **(25)**.

In Scenario A, the attacking midfielder **(17)** makes a dummy movement (checks away) to get free of marking and moves in front of the red No.6 to offer a passing option. The winger **(19)** passes inside and makes a forward run in behind red No.2 to receive the return pass (1-2 combination).

The red full backs (No.2 & No.3) are not fully active, so don't try to tackle the blue players and the red central midfielders (No.6 & No.8) simply follow the blue attacking midfielders' movements.

The practice restarts with the pattern carried out on the right side. Have 2 players in the winger positions to keep the practice at a high tempo.

Scenario B: Give-and-Go with the Defensive Midfielder

Created using SoccerTutor.com Tactics Manager

Description (Scenario B)

In Scenario B, the attacking midfielder **(17)** does not look to provide a passing option for the winger **(19)** in possession.

Instead, the attacking midfielder **(17)** moves diagonally forward as soon as the winger **(19)** receives in the <u>yellow zone</u>. This movement is made to take his marker (red No.6) away.

The defensive midfielder **(25)** moves forward into the available space created by the attacking midfielder's **(17)** forward movement. The winger **(19)** passes diagonally back to the defensive midfielder **(25)**.

Immediately after passing back, the winger **(19)** makes a curved run (to avoid being in an offside position) and receives the aerial pass from the defensive midfielder **(25)** in behind.

In both Scenarios (A and B), the winger receives in a favourable position to cross for team-mates.

The red full backs (No.2 & No.3) are not fully active, so don't try to tackle the blue players and the red central midfielders (No.6 & No.8) simply follow the blue attacking midfielders' movements.

The practice restarts with the pattern carried out on the right side. Have 2 players in the winger positions to keep the practice at a high tempo.

Coaching Points

1. Before the 1-2 combination, the winger should dribble towards the opposing full back but for the give-and-go, he should dribble inside.

2. Quality high speed passing (1 or 2 touches).

3. Well-timed runs by the wingers.

4. Quality low crosses.

5. Well synchronised movements of the players.

PROGRESSION
Practice 3: Combination Play Out Wide in a Dynamic Small Sided Game with End Zone
Scenario A: One-Two Combination with the Attacking Midfielder

Created using SoccerTutor.com Tactics Manager

Description (Scenario A)

In a 35 x 45 yard area, we play an 8 v 7 (+GK) small sided game. Mark out a 10 yard end zone and 2 wide yellow zones. The wide yellow zones are only for the blue wingers **(19 & 7)** and the red full backs (No.2 & No.3).

The blues play against the red players with the aim of moving the ball to the one of the wingers. As soon as the winger **(No.7 in diagram)** receives in the <u>yellow zone</u>, he either plays a 1-2 combination with the attacking midfielder **(8)** or a give-and-go with the defensive midfielder **(25).**

The reaction of the attacking midfielder **(8)** determines what combination is used. In Scenario A, the attacking midfielder **(8)** makes a dummy movement (checks away) to get free of marking and moves in front of the red No.6 to offer a passing option. The winger **(7)** passes inside and makes a forward run in behind the red No.2 to receive the return pass.

If the reds win possession, they try to score in either mini goal. Additionally, if a blue combination is unsuccessful, a coach throws a new ball in for the reds to attack.

PEP GUARDIOLA'S ATTACKING TACTICS

Scenario B: Give-and-Go with the Defensive Midfielder

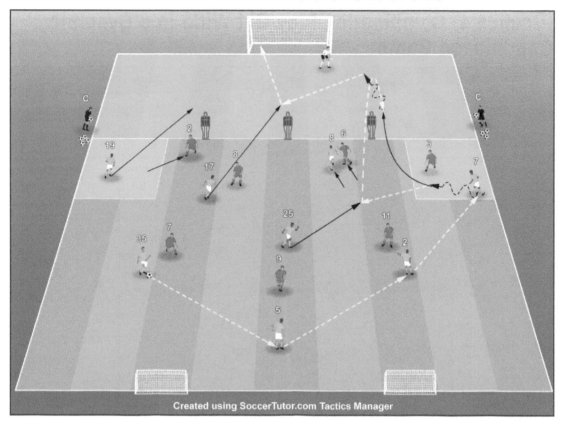

Created using SoccerTutor.com Tactics Manager

Description (Scenario B)

In Scenario B, the attacking midfielder (8) moves diagonally forward as soon as the winger (7) receives in the yellow zone. This movement is made to take away his marker (red No.6).

The defensive midfielder (25) moves forward into the available space created by the attacking midfielder's (8) forward movement. The winger (7) passes diagonally back to the defensive midfielder (25).

Immediately after passing back, the winger (7) makes a curved run (to avoid being in an offside position) and receives the aerial pass from the defensive midfielder (25) in the end zone.

In both Scenarios (A and B), the winger receives in a favourable position to cross for team-mates.

If the reds win possession, they try to score in either mini goal. Additionally, if a blue combination is unsuccessful, a coach throws a new ball in for the reds to attack.

Rules/Restrictions

1. No red players are allowed in the end zone.

2. The red full backs don't try to prevent the wingers from receiving in the yellow zones.

3. If the red team win the ball, the red players can then move freely.

4. The offside rule is applied.

Coaching Point: Before the 1-2 combination, the winger should dribble towards the opposing full back but for the give-and-go, he should dribble inside.

PROGRESSION

Practice 4: Combination Play Out Wide in a Dynamic Conditioned Game

Created using SoccerTutor.com Tactics Manager

Objective: Combination play out wide to break through the opposition's defence.

Description

This is a progression of the previous practice, moving into a 10 v 10 (+GK) game. The blue team start the practice with the centre back **(4)** from the end line.

The blue team can score in any way (1 point), but if they score after a successful 1-2 combination or give-and-go, they score 2 points. Please see the tactical analysis and practices for this tactical situation for both.

In this example, the attacking midfielder **(17)** moves to receive and a 1-2 combination is played.

If the reds win possession, they try to score in either mini goal within 10-12 seconds (2 points).

Rules/Restrictions: A red player can only move into the <u>end zone</u> after the ball is received inside it by a blue player.

Progression: 11v11 in 2/3 of the pitch.

Coaching Points

1. Before the 1-2 combination, the winger should dribble towards the opposing full back but for the give-and-go, he should dribble inside.

2. Good communication and synchronisation between the players (especially the attacking midfielder and winger).

TACTICAL SITUATION 7

Stretching the Opposition's Defence and Switching Play

Content from Analysis of Manchester City during the 2017/2018 and 2018/2019 Premier League winning seasons

The analysis is based on recurring patterns of play observed within the Manchester City team. Once the same phase of play occurred a number of times (at least 10) the tactics would be seen as a pattern. The analysis on the next page is an example of the team's tactics being used effectively, taken from a specific game.

Each action, pass, individual movement with or without the ball, and the positioning of each player on the pitch including their body shape, are presented.

The analysis is then used to create a full progressive session to coach this specific tactical situation.

STRETCHING THE OPPOSITION'S DEFENCE AND SWITCHING PLAY

All the tactical situations so far (Tactical Situations 1-6) can easily be applied against the 4-4-2 and the 4-2-3-1 because the positioning of the opposing No.10 (against the 4-2-3-1) close to City's defensive midfielder **Fernandinho (25)** didn't play a significant role. However, in this tactical situation, an opposing No.10 affects the tactics, so City need different solutions against the 4-2-3-1 than they do against the 4-4-2.

1. Switching Play to the Weak Side After Stretching the Opposition's Defence (Against the 4-4-2)

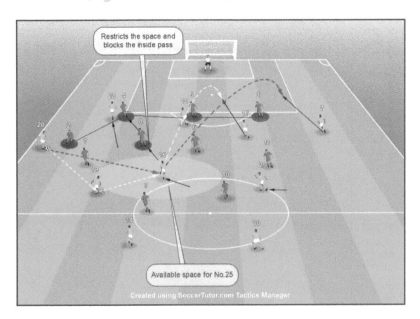

Restricts the space and blocks the inside pass

Available space for No.25

Created using SoccerTutor.com Tactics Manager

The winger **Bernardo (20)** is in possession. The opposing centre back (red No.4) tracks the attacking midfielder **Silva's (21)** run and the opposing central midfielder (red No.8) restricts the space to block the pass to the forward **Agüero (10)**.

However, **Silva's (21)** run and the reaction from red No.4 stretches the opposition's defence and the distances between their defenders increase.

The aim for Pep Guardiola's Manchester City team in this situation is to switch play to the weak side and exploit the available gaps or spaces in the opposition's defence.

The opposing team are using the 4-4-2 formation, so there is space available between the lines.

As the red central midfielder (No.8) has dropped back to prevent the inside pass, the available space in the centre for City's defensive midfielder **Fernandinho (25)** becomes larger.

Options for the City winger **Bernardo (20)**:

1. Move the ball to the defensive midfielder **Fernandinho (25)** via the full back **Delph (18)** - yellow arrows.

2. Pass directly to the defensive midfielder **Fernandinho (25)** - blue arrow.

The available passing options were determined by the positioning and reaction of the opposing full back on the weak side (red No.3).

2. Switching Play to the Weak Side After Stretching the Opposition's Defence (Against the 4-2-3-1)

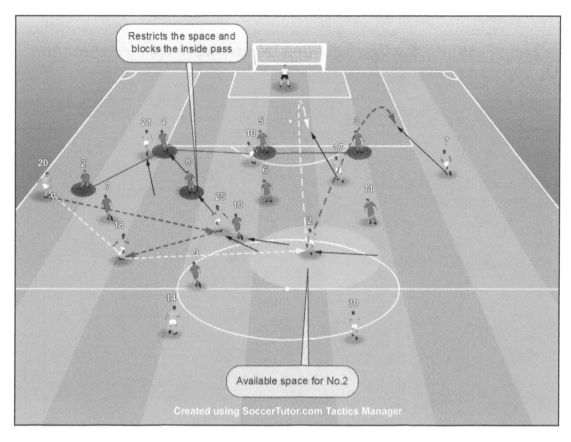

Restricts the space and blocks the inside pass

Available space for No.2

Created using SoccerTutor.com Tactics Manager

This is a variation of the tactical example on the previous page.

When playing against the 4-2-3-1 formation, the space between the lines was controlled by the opposing No.10.

This meant that it was often not possible for Manchester City's defensive midfielder **Fernandinho (25)** to receive free of marking and switch play to the weak side.

In this variation, City's full back on the weak side **Walker (2)** moves into a more central position to take over the role of receiving the ball and switching play.

Options for the City winger **Bernardo (20)**:

1. Move the ball to the right back **Walker (2)** via the left back **Delph (18)** - yellow arrows.

2. Move the ball to the right back **Walker (2)** via the defensive midfielder **Fernandinho (25)** and the left back **Delph (18)** - blue arrows.

There is also an option for the left back **Delph (18)** to pass back to the centre back **Laporte (14)**, who can then pass to **Walker (2)** in the available space.

The available passing options were determined by the positioning and reaction of the opposing full back on the weak side (red No.3).

LONG PASSES INTO THE AVAILABLE SPACE ON THE WEAK SIDE

1. Long Pass into the Gap Between Defenders After Stretching the Opposition's Defence (Against the 4-4-2)

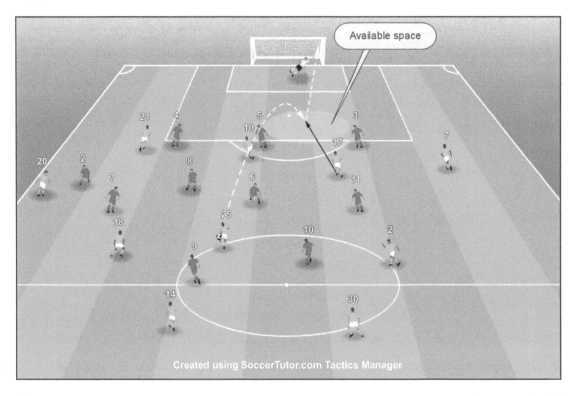

This tactical example shows City playing against the 4-4-2, so the defensive midfielder **Fernandinho (25)** plays the long pass into the most favourable area to create a scoring chance.

As soon as **Fernandinho (25)** receives, the attacking midfielder on the weak side **De Bruyne (17)** moves into the gap between the full back (red No.3) and centre back (red No.5).

If the gap between these 2 opposing defenders was wide enough (as shown in the diagram), **Fernandinho (25)** plays a long pass for **De Bruyne (17)** to receive and try to score.

NOTE:

If Manchester City are playing against the 4-2-3-1 formation, it is the full back **Walker (2)** who plays this pass, but the 2 passing options are the same.

2. Long Pass to the Winger on the Weak Side After Stretching the Opposition's Defence (Against the 4-4-2)

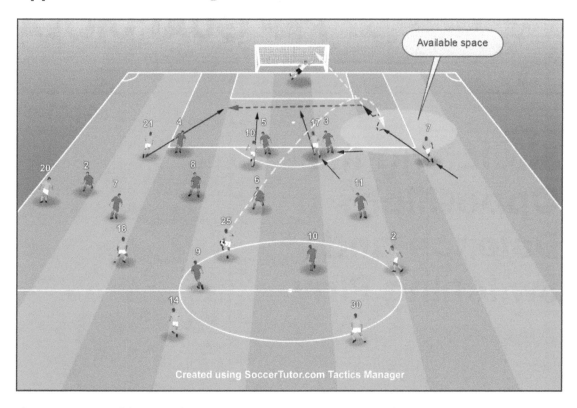

Available space

Created using SoccerTutor.com Tactics Manager

This is a variation of the tactical example shown on the previous page and shows a second option for the defensive midfielder **Fernandinho (25)** after Manchester City have successfully stretched the opposition's defence.

If the attacking midfielder **De Bruyne's (17)** movement to receive in the centre forces the opposing full back (red No.3) to shift across to close the gap and prevent him from receiving a long pass, available space Is then created for the winger **Sterling (7)** in a wider area.

Fernandinho (25) plays a long pass into the available space for **Sterling (7)** to receive in behind and try to score or deliver a low cross for his team-mates, depending on the situation.

NOTE:

The switch of play wasn't only used when the opposition's defence had been stretched, but also in occasions when the opposing defenders had shifted extensively towards the strong side to create a numerical advantage.

This shifting of the opposing defenders created space on the weak side, which was exploited after a quick switch of play just like these last 2 examples.

Stretching the Opposition's Defence and Switching Play

SESSION FOR THIS TACTICAL SITUATION (5 PRACTICES)
Practice 1: Stretching the Opposition's Defence and Switching Play in a Technical Passing Practice
Scenario A: Defensive Midfielder's Long Pass Against the 4-4-2

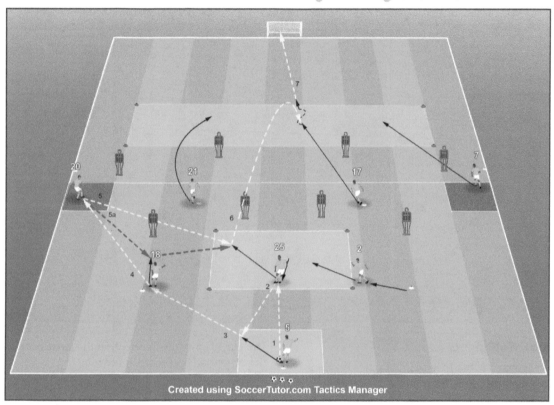

Created using SoccerTutor.com Tactics Manager

Description (Scenario A vs 4-4-2)

In a 50 x 70 yard zone, the centre back **(5)** is inside a white 7 x 3 yard zone, the defensive midfielder **(25)** is inside a yellow 15 x 5 yard zone and the wingers **(20 & 7)** are in 3 x 3 yard wide zones.

The blues use a specific passing pattern. In Scenario A, they move the ball to the defensive midfielder **(25)**, as if playing against the 4-4-2.

When the winger **(20)** receives in the wide blue zone, he can either pass directly to the defensive midfielder **(25)** or via the full back **(18)**.

After receiving within the yellow zone, the defensive midfielder **(25)** has 2 options:

1. Long pass to the attacking midfielder **(17)** in the centre.

2. A wider long pass to the winger **(7)**.

The players must receive within the large zone in the other half and score in the mini goal.

The practice restarts on the right side. There can be 2 players in each position for the 4 advanced players (wingers and attacking midfielders) to keep the practice at a high tempo.

Scenario B: Full Back's Long Pass Against the 4-2-3-1

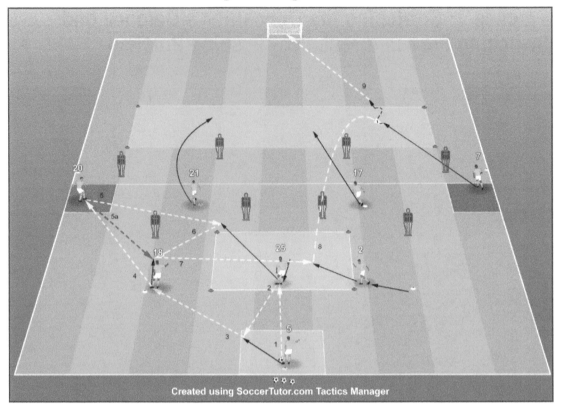

Created using SoccerTutor.com Tactics Manager

Description (Scenario B vs 4-2-3-1)

In Scenario B, the blue team practice playing against the 4-2-3-1 formation.

The ball is instead moved to the full back on the weak side **(2)**, who shifts across to receive and then play the long pass.

When the winger **(20)** receives in the wide blue zone, he can either pass to the defensive midfielder **(25)** or the full back **(18)**. Either way, the ball is moved to the weak side full back **(2)**, as shown in the diagram.

The full back **(2)** has 2 options:

1. Long pass to the attacking midfielder **(17)** in the centre.

2. A wider long pass to the winger **(7)**.

The players must receive within the large zone in the other half and score in the mini goal.

The practice restarts with the pattern carried out on the right side.

There can be 2 players in each position for the 4 advanced players (wingers and attacking midfielders) to keep the practice at a high tempo.

Coaching Points

1. Potential receivers (attacking midfielders and wingers) should time their runs well.

2. Defensive midfielders and full backs need to play accurate long passes into the available space.

PROGRESSION

Practice 2: Stretching the Opposition's Defence and Switching Play in a Tactical Pattern of Play

Scenario A: Defensive Midfielder's Long Pass Against the 4-4-2

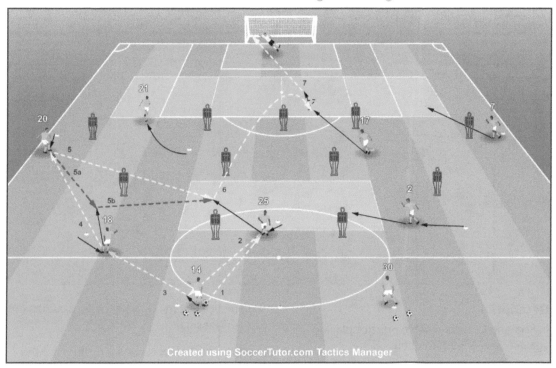

Created using SoccerTutor.com Tactics Manager

Objective: Stretch the defence, switch play, receive in the available space and score.

Description (Scenario A vs 4-4-2)

This is a progression of the previous practice and all the blue players start on the white cones. There are clearly marked zones for the players to receive within.

The blues use a specific passing pattern. In Scenario A, the aim is to move the ball to the defensive midfielder **(25)**, as if playing against the 4-4-2 formation.

When the winger **(20)** receives, he can either pass directly to the defensive midfielder **(25)** in the central zone, or via the full back **(18)**.

After receiving within his zone, the defensive midfielder **(25)** has 2 options:

1. Long pass to the attacking midfielder **(17)** in the central white zone.

2. Long pass to the winger **(7)** in the wide yellow zone.

The player who receives either shoots or crosses for a team-mate to score.

The practice restarts with the pattern carried out on the right side. There can be 2 players in each position for the 4 advanced players (wingers and attacking midfielders) to keep the practice at a high tempo.

PEP GUARDIOLA'S ATTACKING TACTICS

Scenario B: Full Back's Long Pass Against the 4-2-3-1

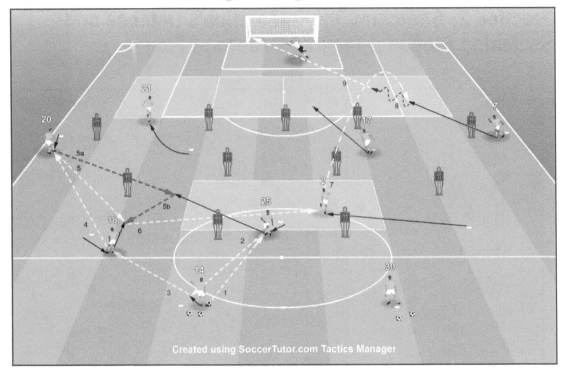

Created using SoccerTutor.com Tactics Manager

Description (Scenario B vs 4-2-3-1)

In Scenario B, the blue team practice playing against the 4-2-3-1 formation.

The ball is instead moved to the full back on the weak side **(2)**, who shifts across to receive and then play the long pass.

When the winger **(20)** receives, he can either pass to the defensive midfielder **(25)** or the full back **(18)**. Either way, the ball is moved to the weak side full back **(2)**, as shown in the diagram.

The full back **(2)** has 2 options:

1. Long pass to the attacking midfielder **(17)** in the central white zone.

2. Long pass to the winger **(7)** in the wider yellow zone.

The player who receives either shoots or crosses for a team-mate to score.

The practice restarts with the pattern carried out on the right side.

There can be 2 players in each position for the 4 advanced players (wingers and attacking midfielders) to keep the practice at a high tempo.

Coaching Points

1. Potential receivers (attacking midfielders and wingers) should time their runs well.

2. Defensive midfielders and full backs need to play accurate long passes into available space.

3. Accurate low crossing and finishing.

4. Well synchronised movements of the players.

PROGRESSION
Practice 3: Stretching the Opposition's Defence and Reading the Attacking Options in a Functional Practice
Scenario A: Defensive Midfielder's Long Pass Against the 4-4-2

Created using SoccerTutor.com Tactics Manager

Description (Scenario A vs 4-4-2)

This is a progression of the previous practice and all the blue players start on the white cones and play against a red back 4.

When the ball reaches the winger on the strong side **(20)**, the red full back No.2 closes him down. The blue attacking midfielder on that side **(21)** makes a diagonal run behind red No.2 and is tracked by the red centre back (No.4).

These reactions leave only red No.5 and No.3 in effective positions. The blues must therefore quickly switch play. As soon as the ball reaches the defensive midfielder **(25)**, the forward **(10)**, the attacking midfielder **(17)** and winger **(7)**

make forward runs into their respective zones.

The defensive midfielder **(25)** has to read the reaction of the red defenders and direct his long pass into the correct area (available space).

In Scenario A, the attacking midfielder **(17)** drags the red full back No.3 with him and space is created out wide for the winger **(7)** to receive the long pass in the wider <u>yellow zone</u>.

If No.3 does not follow blue **No.17**, there is a different option - see Scenario B on next page.

The player who receives either shoots or crosses for a team-mate to score. The practice restarts with the pattern carried out on the right side.

Scenario B: Full Back's Long Pass Against the 4-2-3-1

Created using SoccerTutor.com Tactics Manager

Description (Scenario B vs 4-2-3-1)

In Scenario B, the blue team practice playing against the 4-2-3-1 formation.

The ball is instead moved to the full back on the weak side (2), who shifts across to receive and then play the long pass.

The full back (2) has to read the reaction of the red defenders and direct his long pass into the correct area (available space):

A. If the attacking midfielder (17) drags the red full back No.3 with him, then space is created out wide - see Scenario A on previous page.

B. If the red No.3 does not shift across to close the gap, then there is space available for the attacking midfielder (17) to receive the long pass in the central white zone, as shown in this Scenario B example.

The player who receives either shoots or crosses for a team-mate to score.

The practice restarts with the pattern carried out on the right side

Coaching Points

1. Read the tactical situation: Where has available space been created by the reactions of the opposing defenders?

2. Quality and accurate long passing.

3. Accurate low crossing and finishing.

PROGRESSION
Practice 4: Stretching the Opposition's Defence and Reading the Attacking Options in a Zonal Game
Scenario A: Defensive Midfielder's Long Pass Against the 4-4-2

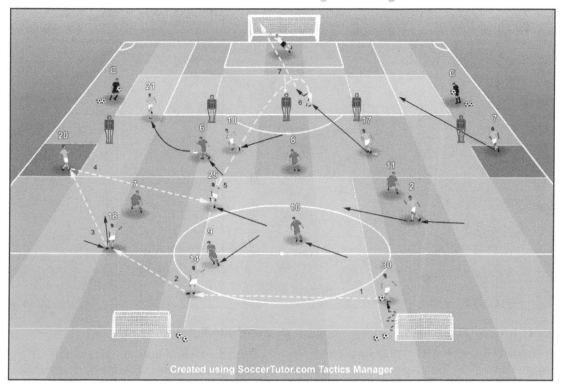

Created using SoccerTutor.com Tactics Manager

Description (Scenario A vs 4-4-2)

This is a progression of the previous practice and the blue team must now switch play under pressure from the red midfielders and forwards.

We add 2 wide blue zones for the wingers (20 & 7) and a white central white zone, where the red wide midfielder on the weak side (No.11 in diagram example) cannot enter.

The blue team start the game with the centre back (30) and a 5 v 4 situation in the lower part of the pitch against the 2 red forwards and 2 wide midfielders. However, the 2 red central midfielders can also move into this part.

The blues have 2 options:

1. Switch play to the weak side.
2. Pass inside to the forward (10).

The possibility of the pass to the forward (10) means red No.6 drop backs, which creates space in the centre to be exploited by the defensive midfielder (25), who receives and switches play.

The player who receives either shoots or crosses. If the reds win the ball or a switch of play is inaccurate (not within zones), a coach throws a new ball in for the reds to try and score in the 2 mini goals.

Scenario B: Full Back's Long Pass Against the 4-2-3-1

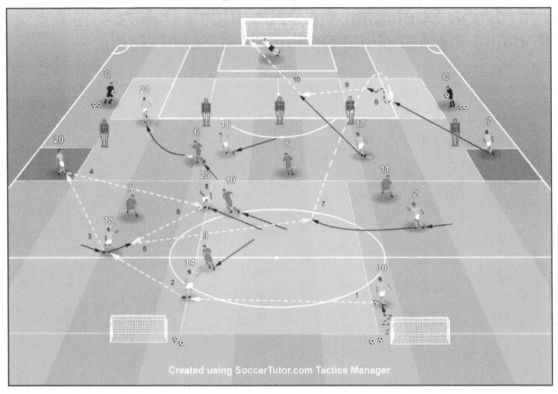

Created using SoccerTutor.com Tactics Manager

Description (Scenario B vs 4-2-3-1)

In Scenario B, the blue team practice playing against the 4-2-3-1 formation.

This is different to Scenario A on the previous page, as the opposition's No.10 prevents the defensive midfielder **(25)** from receiving so easily in space.

If the pass to the forward **(10)** is blocked by red No.6, the ball is instead moved to the full back on the weak side **(2)**, who shifts across to receive and then play the long pass.

The player who receives the long pass either shoots or crosses for a team-mate to score.

If the reds win the ball or a switch of play is inaccurate (not within zones), a coach throws a new ball in for the reds to try and score in the 2 mini goals.

Coaching Points

1. Read the tactical situation: Where has available space been created by the reactions of the opposing defenders?
2. Quality high speed passing (1 or 2 touches).
3. Quality and accurate long passing.
4. Accurate low crossing and finishing.
5. Well synchronised movements of the players.

Progression: Add 4 red defenders and play a 10 v 10 (+GK) game.

PROGRESSION

Practice 5: Stretching the Opposition's Defence and Reading the Attacking Options in a Conditioned Game

Created using SoccerTutor.com Tactics Manager

Objective: Stretch the defence, switch play, receive in the available space and score.

Description

In this final practice of the session, the 2 teams play a conditioned 11v11 game. The practice starts from the blue team's goalkeeper.

The blue team can score in any way (1 point), but if they score after stretching the opposition's defence and switching play, they score 2 points. Please see all practices in this session for different ways the blues attack in this situation.

If the reds win possession, they try to score within 12-15 seconds (2 points).

Variation: Adjust to play against the 4-2-3-1, with the full back receiving and playing the long pass - see Scenario B in all previous practices.

Coaching Points

1. Read the tactical situation: Does the winger pass directly to the defensive midfielder or pass to the full back?

2. Read the tactical situation: Where is best to direct the long pass? Where is the available space?

3. Quality high speed passing (1 or 2 touches).

4. Quality and accurate long passing.

TACTICAL SITUATION 8

Attacking Options when the Attacking Midfielder Receives Between the Lines

Content from Analysis of Manchester City during the 2017/2018 and 2018/2019 Premier League winning seasons

The analysis is based on recurring patterns of play observed within the Manchester City team. Once the same phase of play occurred a number of times (at least 10) the tactics would be seen as a pattern. The analysis on the next page is an example of the team's tactics being used effectively, taken from a specific game.

Each action, pass, individual movement with or without the ball, and the positioning of each player on the pitch including their body shape, are presented.

The analysis is then used to create a full progressive session to coach this specific tactical situation.

ATTACKING MIDFIELDERS MOVE INTO AVAILABLE PASSING LANES TO RECEIVE

Both Attacking Midfielders Move into Available Passing Lanes to Receive from the Defensive Midfielder

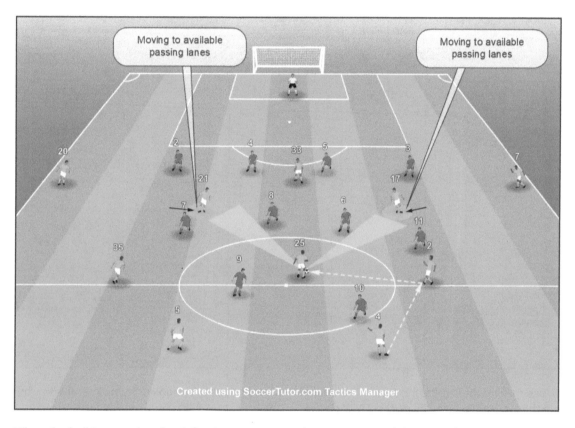

When the ball is moved to the defensive midfielder **Fernandinho (25)**, there is always the option of attacking through the centre.

Pep Guardiola has both his Manchester City attacking midfielders move towards the available passing lanes to receive (inside movement).

In this example, **Silva (21)** and **De Bruyne (17)** are the attacking midfielders. **Bernardo (20)** and **Gündoğan (8)** have also often played in these positions.

The positioning of the 2 attacking midfielders in the space between the zone of responsibility of the opposing centre back and full back made it difficult for the opposition to control them.

In this example, the defensive midfielder **Fernandinho (25)** has time, space and available passing lanes to pass to either attacking midfielder **Silva (21)** or **De Bruyne (17)**.

RECEIVING THE BALL WITH AN OPEN BODY SHAPE (ON THE HALF-TURN)

Attacking Midfielders Receive on the Half-Turn Between the Lines

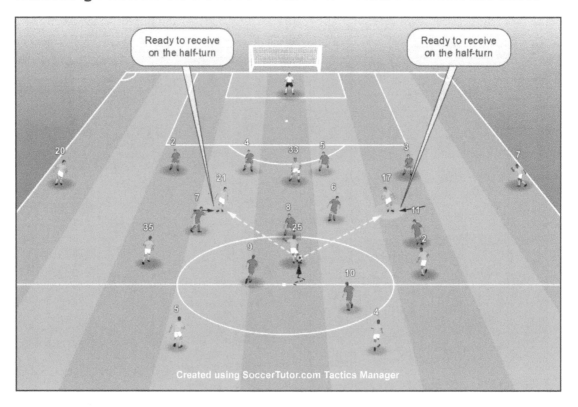

When making their inside movements to open up the available passing lanes, the 2 Manchester City attacking midfielders used a good open body shape.

This body shape enabled them to receive on the half-turn and then move quickly forward facing the opposition's goal.

ATTACKING OPTIONS AFTER RECEIVING BETWEEN THE LINES (READING REACTION OF FULL BACK)

1. Opposing Full Back Stays Back: Receive, Turn and Pass in Behind

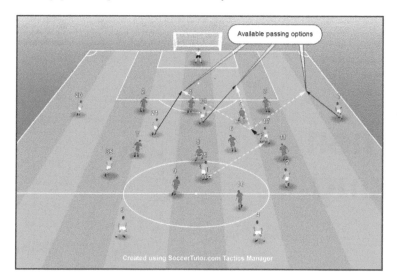

As soon as the attacking midfielder **De Bruyne (17)** receives free of marking, he is able to move forward facing the opposition's goal. This is because the opposing full back (red No.3) stays back to retain balance in the defensive line.

In this situation, City have a 5v4 advantage for their attack. **De Bruyne (17)** can play a key pass for one of his team-mates or shoot at goal.

2. Opposing Full Back Presses Attacking Midfielder: Lay-Off for Defensive Midfielder's Aerial Pass to the Winger

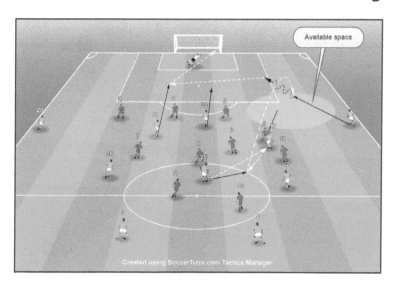

In this variation of the previous example, the opposing full back (red No.3) moves forward to press the attacking midfielder **De Bruyne (17)** and this creates in behind.

The ball is played to **Sterling (7)** after **De Bruyne (17)** lays the ball back to the defensive midfielder **Fernandinho (25)**, who then plays an aerial pass into the available space created.

Attacking Options when the Attacking Midfielder Receives Between the Lines

Practice 1: Attacking Options when the Attacking Midfielder Receives Between the Lines in a Passing Practice

Scenario A: Strong Side Attacking Midfielder Receives Unmarked

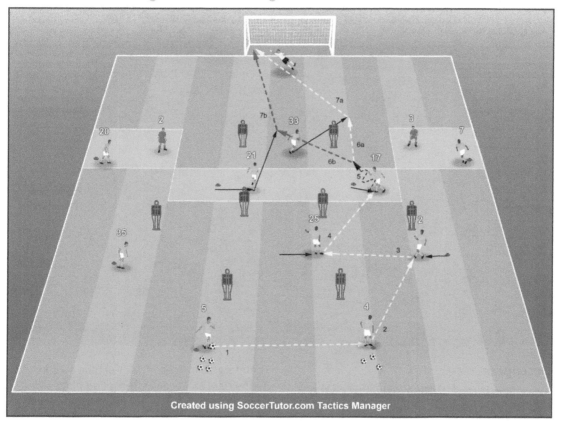

Created using SoccerTutor.com Tactics Manager

Description (Scenario A)

In a 35 x 45 yard area, the practice starts with the centre back **(5)**. There is a 20 x 5 yard white central zone for the blue attacking midfielders **(21 & 17)** and two 8 x 5 yard yellow wide zones for the blue wingers **(20 & 7)** and red full backs.

The blue back 4 pass amongst themselves. As soon as the defensive midfielder **(25)** receives in between the lines with an open body shape (half-turn), the attacking midfielders **(21 & 17)** move towards the available passing lanes to receive.

The defensive midfielder **(25)** passes to one of the attacking midfielders **(No.17 on the strong side in diagram)** and he has to read the reaction of the opposing full back (red No.3).

In Scenario A, the attacking midfielder **(17)** receives within the white central zone and the red full back on that side (No.3) stays in the wide yellow zone, so the blue attacking midfielder **(17)** receives, turns and plays a key pass.

Scenario B: Weak Side Attacking Midfielder Receives Unmarked

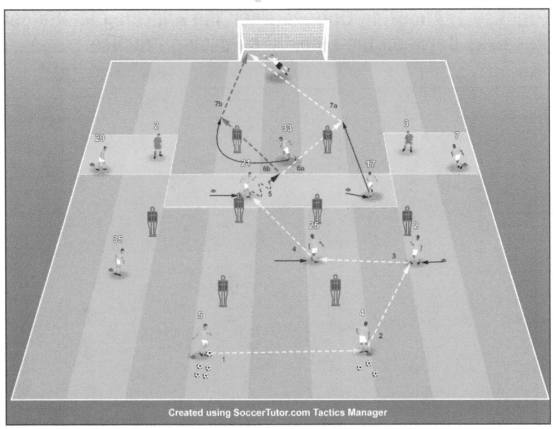

Description (Scenario B)

In Scenario B, the attacking midfielder on the weak side **(21)** receives from the defensive midfielder **(25)** within the white central zone and the red full back on that side (No.3) stays in the wide yellow zone.

Therefore, as in Scenario A, the blue attacking midfielder **(21)** receives, turns and plays a key pass.

Scenario C: Opposing Full Back Prevents Strong Side AM Turning

Created using SoccerTutor.com Tactics Manager

Description (Scenario C)

In Scenario C, the attacking midfielder on the strong side **(17)** receives from the defensive midfielder **(25)** and the red full back on that side (No.3) moves forward into the <u>white central zone</u> to prevent him from turning.

This creates space in behind for the winger **(7)** to receive unmarked.

The ball is played to the winger **(7)** after the attacking midfielder **(17)** lays the ball back to the defensive midfielder **(25)**, who then plays an aerial pass into the available space created.

The winger **(7)** can either shoot at goal or cross for a team-mate to score.

Scenario D: Opposing Full Back Prevents Weak Side AM Turning

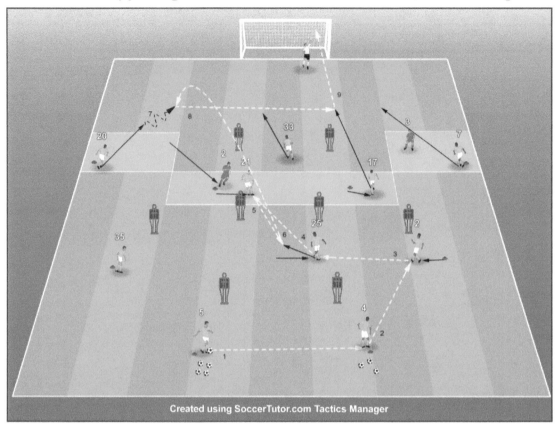

Created using SoccerTutor.com Tactics Manager

Description (Scenario D)

In Scenario D, the attacking midfielder on the weak side **(21)** receives from the defensive midfielder **(25)** and the red full back on that side (No.2) moves forward into the <u>white central zone</u> to prevent him from turning.

This creates space in behind for the winger **(20)** to receive unmarked.

The ball is played to the winger **(20)** after the attacking midfielder **(17)** lays the ball back to the defensive midfielder **(25)**, who then plays an aerial pass into the available space created.

The winger **(20)** can either shoot at goal or cross for a team-mate to score.

Coaching Points

1. Read the tactical situation: The attacking midfielder **(21 or 17)** must read the reaction of the opposing full back to know whether to turn or lay the ball back to the defensive midfielder **(25)**.

2. Receive with an open body shape and turn quickly.

3. Quality high speed passing (1 or 2 touches).

4. Quality low crossing and accurate finishing.

5. Well-timed runs in behind (not offside).

PROGRESSION

Practice 2: Attacking Options when the Attacking Midfielder Receives Between the Lines in a Functional Practice

Scenario A: Attacking Midfielder Receives Unmarked

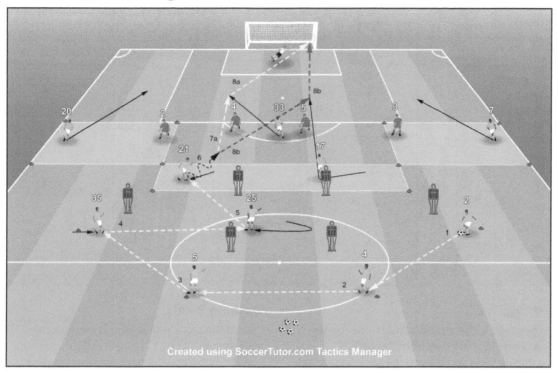

Created using SoccerTutor.com Tactics Manager

Objective: Attacking options for the attacking midfielder after receiving between the lines.

Description (Scenario A)

This is a progression of the previous practice and the blues play against a red back 4. There is a 30 x 5 yard white central zone for the blue attacking midfielders **(21 & 17)** and two 12 x 8 yard yellow wide zones for the blue wingers **(20 & 7)** and red full backs (No.2 & No.3).

The blue back 4 pass amongst themselves. As soon as the defensive midfielder **(25)** receives in between the lines with an open body shape, the attacking midfielders **(21 & 17)** move towards the available passing lanes to receive.

The defensive midfielder **(25)** passes to one of the attacking midfielders **(No.21 on the strong side in diagram)** and he has to read the reaction of the opposing full back on that side (red No.2).

In Scenario A, the attacking midfielder **(21)** receives within the white central zone and the red full back on that side (No.3) stays in the wide yellow zone, so the blue attacking midfielder **(21)** receives, turns and plays a key pass.

Scenario B: Opposing Full Back Prevents AM from Turning

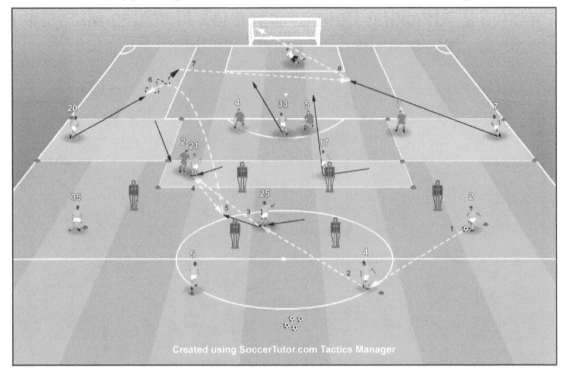

Created using SoccerTutor.com Tactics Manager

Description (Scenario B)

In Scenario B, the attacking midfielder on the weak side **(21)** receives from the defensive midfielder **(25)** and the red full back on that side (No.2) moves forward into the <u>white central zone</u> to prevent him from turning.

This creates space in behind for the winger **(20)** to receive unmarked.

The ball is played to the winger **(20)** after the attacking midfielder **(21)** lays the ball back to the defensive midfielder **(25)**, who then plays an aerial pass into the available space created.

The winger **(20)** crosses for a team-mate to score.

Coaching Points

1. Read the tactical situation: The attacking midfielder **(21 or 17)** must read the reaction of the opposing full back to know whether to turn or lay the ball back to the defensive midfielder **(25)**.

2. Receive with an open body shape and turn quickly.

3. Quality high speed passing (1 or 2 touches).

4. Quality low crossing and accurate finishing.

5. Well-timed runs in behind (not offside).

PROGRESSION

Practice 3: Attacking Options when the Attacking Midfielder Receives Between the Lines in a Conditioned Game

Created using SoccerTutor.com Tactics Manager

Objective: Attacking options for the attacking midfielder after receiving between the lines.

Description

This is a progression of the previous practice, moving into a 10 v 10 (+GK) game. The blue team start the practice with the centre back **(5)** from the end line.

The blue team can score in any way (1 point), but if they score after the defensive midfielder **(25)** successfully passes to one of the attacking midfielders **(21 or 17)** between the lines, they score 2 points.

Please see the tactical analysis and practices for all possible situations, reactions and options.

If the reds win possession, they try to score in either mini goal within 10-12 seconds (2 points).

The marked zones are only used to make it easier for the blues to read the tactical situation and can be removed.

Rule/Restriction: Only the red full backs can move inside the white central zone to prevent the blue attacking midfielders **(21 or 17)** from turning.

TACTICAL SITUATION 9

Exploiting Space Created when the Opposing Centre Back Pushes Out to Press the Ball

Content from Analysis of Manchester City during the 2017/2018 and 2018/2019 Premier League winning seasons

The analysis is based on recurring patterns of play observed within the Manchester City team. Once the same phase of play occurred a number of times (at least 10) the tactics would be seen as a pattern. The analysis on the next page is an example of the team's tactics being used effectively, taken from a specific game.

Each action, pass, individual movement with or without the ball, and the positioning of each player on the pitch including their body shape, are presented.

The analysis is then used to create a full progressive session to coach this specific tactical situation.

EXPLOITING SPACE CREATED WHEN THE OPPOSING CENTRE BACK PUSHES OUT TO PRESS THE BALL

1. Opposing Centre Back Pushes Out to Press Attacking Midfielder in a Wide Position: Pass into Available Space for Forward

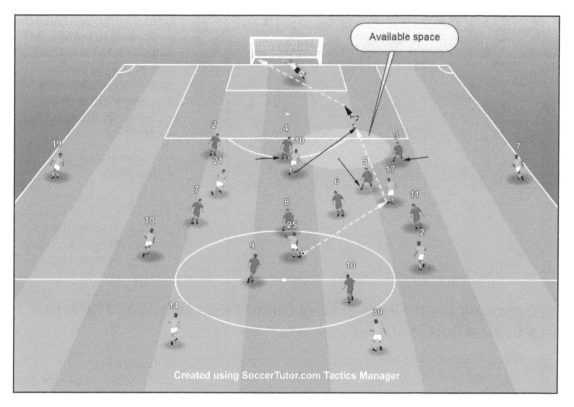

Available space

Created using SoccerTutor.com Tactics Manager

In this tactical situation, the defensive midfielder **Fernandinho (25)** is in possession and is looking to pass to one of the attacking midfielders in between the lines, as in the previous "Tactical Situation 8."

Fernandinho (25) passes to the attacking midfielder **(De Bruyne - 17 in diagram)** in a wide position. If the opposing centre back (red No.5) moves out of the defensive line to close down the attacking midfielder, **De Bruyne's (17)** open body shape allows him to see red No.5's movement.

As the diagonal pass to the forward **Agüero (10)** is blocked and the red centre back (No.4) has approached at a diagonal angle due to the attacking midfielder **De Bruyne's (17)** wide position, the best option is a vertical pass into the space created in behind.

The quick reading of the situation and the communication between the forward **Agüero (10)** and the attacking midfielder **De Bruyne (17)** results in **Agüero (10)** receiving in behind with a good chance to score.

PEP GUARDIOLA'S ATTACKING TACTICS

2. Opposing Centre Back Pushes Out to Press Attacking Midfielder in a Central Position: 1-2 Combination to Receive in Available Space

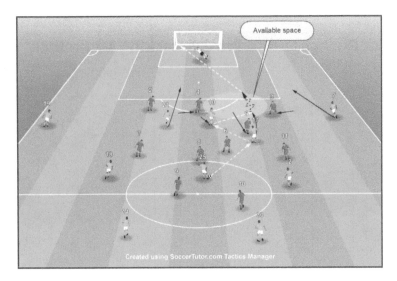

If the attacking midfielder **De Bruyne (17)** was positioned more centrally, the opposing centre back (red No.5) used a straight/vertical run to close him down. This prevented the vertical pass to the forward **Agüero (10)** shown in the example on the previous page. In this situation, the Manchester City attacking midfielder **De Bruyne (17)** would either:

1. Receive and turn if possible.

2. Play a 1-2 combination with the forward **Agüero (10)** and receive the return pass in the space created (as shown in the diagram).

3. Opposing Centre Back Pushes Out to Press Attacking Midfielder in a Central Position: Pass Inside for Team-mate to Play to Forward

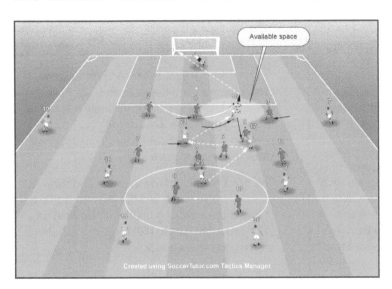

In this variation of the previous example, **De Bruyne (17)** passes inside to the other attacking midfielder **Silva (21)** instead of the forward.

The forward **Agüero (10)** moves into the available space behind red No.5 using a curved run.

Silva (21) plays a first time pass into the available space for **Agüero (10)** to receive on the run, with a great scoring chance.

Exploiting Space Created when the Opposing Centre Back Pushes Out to Press the Ball

Practice 1: Exploiting Space Created when the Centre Back Pushes Out to Press Ball (Unopposed)

Scenario A: The Attacking Midfielder Receives in a Wide Position

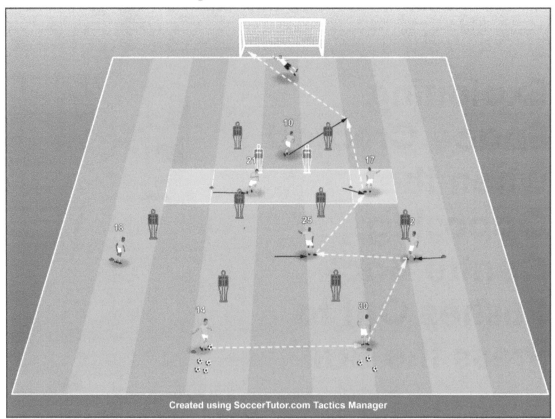

Created using SoccerTutor.com Tactics Manager

Description (Scenario A)

In a 35 x 45 yard area, the practice starts with the centre back **(14)**. There is a 12 x 5 yard white central zone and two 4 x 5 yard yellow wide zones for the blue attacking midfielders.

The blue back 4 pass amongst themselves. As soon as the defensive midfielder **(25)** receives in between the lines with an open body shape (half-turn), the attacking midfielders **(21 & 17)** move towards the available passing lanes to receive.

The defensive midfielder **(25)** passes to one of the attacking midfielders **(21 or 17)**.

In Scenario A, we imagine the opposing centre back moves to press the blue attacking midfielder **(17)** at a diagonal angle, due to his wide position. This opens up a vertical passing lane to the forward **(10)** into the created space. The forward **(10)** receives and tries to score.

The attacking midfielder **(17)** is limited to 2 touches (receive and pass).

Scenario B: The Attacking Midfielder Receives in a Central Position

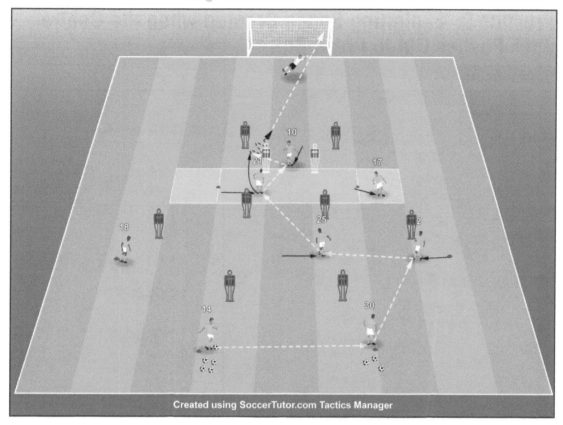

Created using SoccerTutor.com Tactics Manager

Description (Scenario B)

In Scenario B, the attacking midfielder **(No.21 in diagram example)** receives the pass in the white central zone.

We imagine the opposing centre back moves to press the blue attacking midfielder **(21)** at a straight/vertical angle, due to his central position.

This means that the vertical pass to the forward **(10)**, as shown in Scenario A, is no longer an option.

The attacking midfielder **(21)** therefore plays a 1-2 combination with the forward **(10)** and receives the return pass ahead of the white mannequin. He then tries to score.

Coaching Points

1. Read the tactical situation: The forward moves according to whether the attacking midfielder receives in a central or wide position.

2. Receive with an open body shape and turn quickly.

3. Quality high speed passing (1 or 2 touches).

4. Quality and accurate finishing.

5. Well-timed runs of the players.

PROGRESSION

Practice 2: Exploiting Space Created when the Centre Back Pushes Out to Press Ball (Opposed)

Scenario A: The Attacking Midfielder Receives in a Wide Position

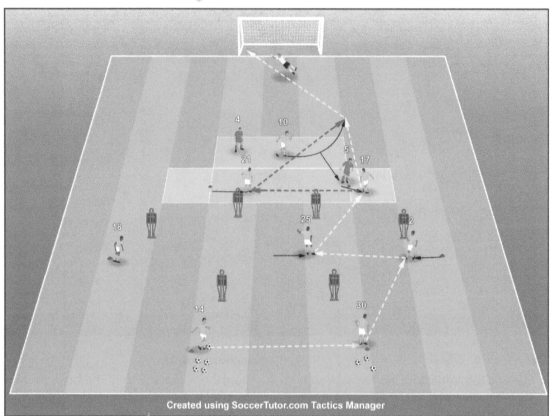

Created using SoccerTutor.com Tactics Manager

Description (Scenario A)

This is a progression of the previous practice, with 2 red centre backs (No.4 and No.5) added.

The blue back 4 pass amongst themselves. As soon as the defensive midfielder **(25)** receives, the attacking midfielders **(21 & 17)** move into the available passing lanes to receive in either the white central zone or a wide yellow zone.

The respective red centre back moves forward to close down the blue attacking midfielder **(No.17 in diagram)**.

In Scenario A, the red centre back No.5 moves to press the blue attacking midfielder **(17)** at a diagonal angle due to his wide position.

The attacking midfielder **(17)** has 2 options:

1. If there is time and space, receive and pass forward (vertical) in behind to the forward **(10)**, using a maximum of 2 touches.

2. If the vertical pass is blocked, pass inside to the other attacking midfielder **(21)**, who then passes to the forward **(10)** - see blue arrows.

PEP GUARDIOLA'S ATTACKING TACTICS

Scenario B: The Attacking Midfielder Receives in a Central Position

Created using SoccerTutor.com Tactics Manager

Description (Scenario B)

In Scenario B, the red centre back (No.4) moves to press the blue attacking midfielder **(21)** at a straight/vertical angle due to his central position.

This means that the vertical pass to the forward **(10)**, as shown in Scenario A, is no longer an option.

The attacking midfielder **(21)** therefore plays a 1-2 combination with the forward **(10)** and receives the return pass in the space created in behind. He then tries to score.

Coaching Points

1. Read the tactical situation: The forward moves according to whether the attacking midfielder receives in the centre or wide and the opposing centre back's reaction.

2. Receive with an open body shape and turn quickly.

3. Quality high speed passing (1 or 2 touches).

4. Quality and accurate finishing.

5. Well-timed runs of the players.

PROGRESSION

Practice 3: Exploiting Space Created when the Centre Back Pushes Out to Press Ball in a Functional Practice

Scenario A: The Attacking Midfielder Receives in a Wide Position

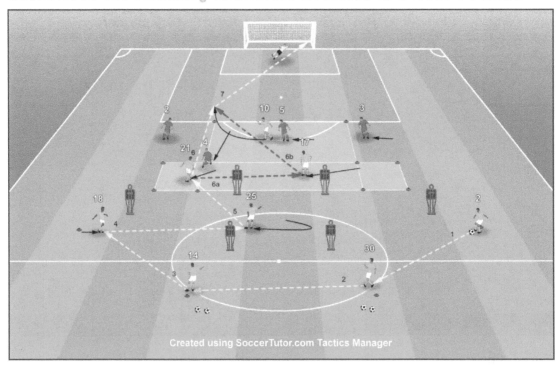

Created using SoccerTutor.com Tactics Manager

Description (Scenario A)

This is a progression of the previous practice and the blues play against a red back 4.

The blue back 4 pass amongst themselves. As soon as the defensive midfielder **(25)** receives, the attacking midfielders **(21 & 17)** move into the available passing lanes to receive in either the <u>white central zone</u> or a <u>wide yellow zone</u>.

The respective red centre back (No.4 in diagram) moves forward to close down the blue attacking midfielder **(No.21 in diagram)**.

Restriction/Rule: The red full backs (No.2 & No.3) defend normally but they are not allowed to enter any of the zones at any time.

In Scenario A, the red centre back (No.4) moves to press the blue attacking midfielder **(21)** at a diagonal angle due to his wide position.

The attacking midfielder **(21)** has 2 options:

1. If there is time and space, receive and pass forward (vertical) in behind to the forward **(10)**, using a maximum of 2 touches.

2. If the vertical pass is blocked, pass inside to the other attacking midfielder **(17)**, who then passes to the forward **(10)** - see blue arrows.

Scenario B: The Attacking Midfielder Receives in a Central Position

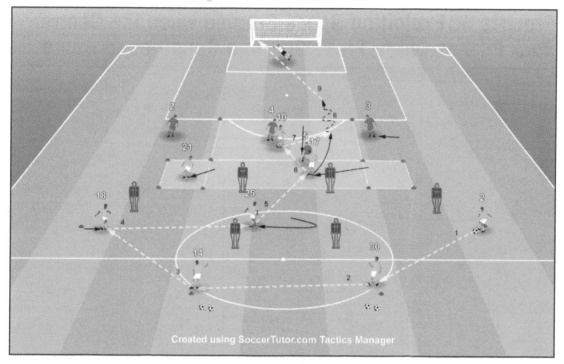

Created using SoccerTutor.com Tactics Manager

Description (Scenario B)

In Scenario B, the red centre back (No.5) moves to press the blue attacking midfielder **(17)** at a straight/vertical angle due to his central position.

This means that the vertical pass to the forward **(10)**, as shown in Scenario A, is no longer an option.

The attacking midfielder **(17)** therefore plays a 1-2 combination with the forward **(10)** and receives the return pass in the space created in behind. He then tries to score.

Coaching Points

1. Read the tactical situation: The forward moves according to whether the attacking midfielder receives in the centre or wide and the opposing centre back's reaction.

2. Receive with an open body shape and turn quickly.

3. Quality high speed passing (1 or 2 touches).

4. Quality and accurate finishing.

5. Well-timed runs of the players.

PROGRESSION

Practice 4: Exploiting Space Created when the Centre Back Pushes Out to Press Ball in a Conditioned Game

Created using SoccerTutor.com Tactics Manager

Description

This is a progression of the previous practice, moving into a 10 v 10 (+GK) game. The blue team start the practice with the centre back **(30)** from the end line.

The blue team can score in any way (1 point), but if they score after the defensive midfielder **(25)** passes to one of the attacking midfielders **(21 or 17)** and then exploit the space created by the opposing centre back pushing out, they score 2 points.

Please see the tactical analysis and practices for all possible situations, reactions and options.

If the reds win possession, they try to score in either mini goal within 10-12 seconds (2 points).

The marked zones are only used to make it easier for the blues to read the tactical situation and can be removed.

Restrictions/Rules

1. The red full backs (No.2 & No.3) are not allowed to enter any of the zones at any time.

2. The red centre backs (No.4 & No.5) are coached to put pressure on the attacking midfielders within the zones.

Progression

11v11 game in 2/3 of the pitch with the same aims and without any marked out zones.

TACTICAL SITUATION 10

Attacking Through the Centre with the Forward Dropping Back to Receive

Content from Analysis of Manchester City during the 2017/2018 and 2018/2019 Premier League winning seasons

The analysis is based on recurring patterns of play observed within the Manchester City team. Once the same phase of play occurred a number of times (at least 10) the tactics would be seen as a pattern. The analysis on the next page is an example of the team's tactics being used effectively, taken from a specific game.

Each action, pass, individual movement with or without the ball, and the positioning of each player on the pitch including their body shape, are presented.

The analysis is then used to create a full progressive session to coach this specific tactical situation.

ATTACKING THROUGH THE CENTRE WITH THE FORWARD DROPPING BACK TO RECEIVE

1. Forward Drops Back to Become a Link Player and Create Space in Behind to Move the Ball to the Attacking Midfielder

When it wasn't possible for the defensive midfielder **Fernandinho (25)** to pass to the attacking midfielders **(21 & 17)**, the forward **(Jesus - 33 in diagram example)** dropped back to become a link player and direct the ball to them.

The forward **Jesus (33)** notices that the pass towards the attacking midfielder **De Bruyne (17)** is not easy, so he drops a few yards back to provide a passing option and become the link player to move the ball to the attacking midfielder on the strong side.

De Bruyne (17) receives facing the opposition's goal and a 2v1 situation is created on the right side, with **De Bruyne (17)** and the winger **Bernardo (20)** against the red full back No.3.

The attacking midfielder **De Bruyne (17)** has 2 options:

1. Dribble forward to exploit the free space behind the red centre back (No.5) and shoot.

2. Pass out wide to the right winger **Bernardo (20)**, who will most likely deliver a low cross for a team-mate - see blue arrows.

PEP GUARDIOLA'S ATTACKING TACTICS

2. Forward Drops Back to Become a Link Player and Manchester City Use a Third Man Run Combination to Receive in Behind

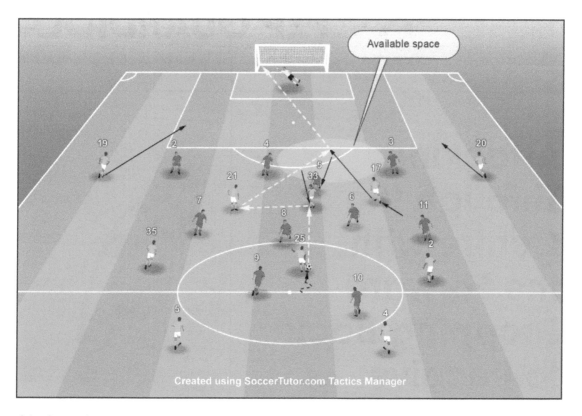

Created using SoccerTutor.com Tactics Manager

If the forward **Jesus (33)** passes to the attacking midfielder on the weak side **Silva (21)**, a 2v2 situation is created on the left side.

In this situation, the available space behind the red centre back (No.5) can be best exploited with the third man run of the other attacking midfielder **De Bruyne (17)**.

As soon as the pass from the forward **Jesus (33)** to **Silva (21)** is played, **De Bruyne (17)** starts his forward movement towards the available space behind red No.5.

A diagonal first time pass from **Silva (21)** is played into **De Bruyne's (17)** path, he receives on the run and shoots at goal.

NOTE:

A decisive element that determines which attacking midfielder the forward passes to is his body shape and which side he is angled towards

If the forward is half-turned towards the attacking midfielder on the weak side **(21)**, then the attacking midfielder on the strong side **(17)** should be ready to start his diagonal run as soon as the ball reaches the forward's **(33)** feet.

Attacking Through the Centre with the Forward Dropping Back to Receive

SESSION FOR THIS TACTICAL SITUATION (2 PRACTICES)

Practice 1: Attacking Through the Centre with the Forward Dropping Back in a Functional Practice

Scenario A: Forward Passes to Attacking Midfielder on Strong Side

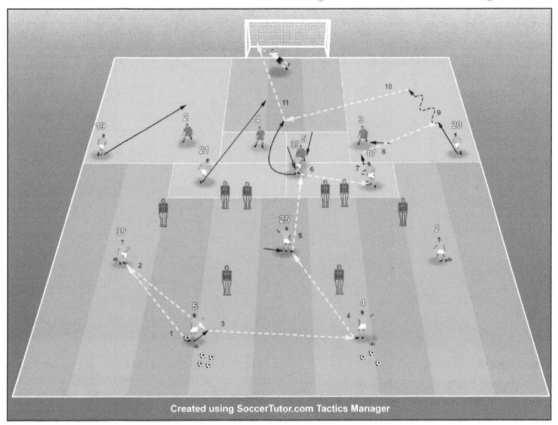

Created using SoccerTutor.com Tactics Manager

Description (Scenario A)

In a 35 x 45 yard area, the practice starts with the centre back **(5)**. There is a low 20 x 5 yard white central zone and a high 12 x 5 yard white central zone - both are divided in half vertically.

There are also two 12 x 20 yard yellow wide zones for the blue wingers **(19 & 20)** and the red full backs (No.2 & No.3).

The blue back 4 pass amongst themselves. The passing lanes to the attacking midfielders **(21 & 17)** are blocked, so as soon as the defensive

midfielder **(25)** receives, the forward **(10)** drops back into the low white central zone and becomes a link player to move the ball to them.

In Scenario A, the forward **(10)** passes to the attacking midfielder on the strong side **(17)**, who has 2 options:

1. Dribble forward to exploit the free space behind the red centre back (No.5) and shoot.

2. Pass out wide to the right winger **(20)** in the yellow wide zone who delivers a low cross for oncoming team-mates - see diagram example.

Scenario B: Forward Passes to Attacking Midfielder on Weak Side

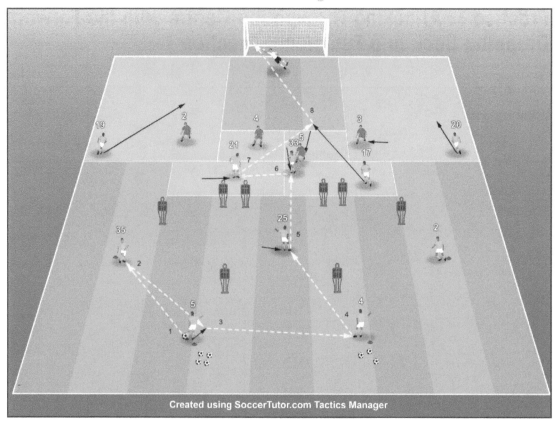

Created using SoccerTutor.com Tactics Manager

Description (Scenario B)

In Scenario B, the forward **(33)** passes to the attacking midfielder on the weak side **(21)**, so a 2v2 situation is created on the left side.

The available space behind the red centre back (No.5) is best exploited with the third man run of the other attacking midfielder **(17)**.

As soon as the pass from the forward **(33)** to the attacking midfielder on the weak side **(21)** is played, the attacking midfielder on the strong side **(17)** starts his forward movement towards the available space behind red No.5.

A diagonal first time pass from **No.21** is played into **No.17's** path - he receives on the run and shoots at goal.

Repeat with the forward **(33)** receiving on the other side with the other red centre back (No.4) moving to close him down. **No.21** becomes the attacking midfielder on the new strong side and **No.17** on the new weak side.

Coaching Points

1. Read the tactical situation: Is the ball passed to the attacking midfielder on the strong side or the attacking midfielder on the weak side?

2. Receive with an open body shape and turn quickly.

3. Quality high speed passing (1 or 2 touches).

4. Quality and accurate finishing.

5. Well-timed runs of the players.

PROGRESSION

Practice 2: Attacking Through the Centre with the Forward Dropping Back in a Dynamic Conditioned Game

Created using SoccerTutor.com Tactics Manager

Description

This is a progression of the previous practice, moving into a 10 v 10 (+GK) game. The blue team start the practice with the centre back **(4)** from the end line.

The blue team can score in any way (1 point), but if they score after passing to the forward who drops back and combine to overcome the pressing of the opposing centre back, they score 2 points. Please see the analysis and practices for all possible situations, reactions and options.

In this example, the forward **(33)** passes to the attacking midfielder on the strong side **(21)**, who can either dribble forward and shoot or pass to the winger **(19)**.

If the reds win possession, they try to score in either mini goal within 10-12 seconds (2 points).

The marked zones are only used to make it easier for the blues to read the tactical situation and can be removed.

Restrictions/Rules

1. The red full backs are not allowed to enter the central zones at any time.

2. The red centre backs are coached to put pressure on the attacking midfielders within their zones.

Progression: 11v11 game in 2/3 of the pitch with the same aims and without any zones.

PEP GUARDIOLA'S ATTACKING TACTICS

ATTACKING AGAINST THE 4-3-3

ATTACKING AGAINST THE 4-3-3

When a Manchester City attacking midfielder **(No.17 in diagram below)** makes a diagonal run in behind the opposing full back (red No.2) against the 4-3-3 formation, it was the opposing defensive midfielder (No.6) who shifted across to block the potential inside pass by the City winger **(No.19 in diagram)**.

Space between the lines is restricted as there are 2 opposing attacking midfielders (No.8 &

No.10), so the defensive midfielder **Fernandinho (25)** was usually marked or the passing lane to him was blocked by the strong side's attacking midfielder (No.8). This meant the direct pass from the winger **Sané (19)** to the defensive midfielder **Fernandinho (25)** was not possible.

Against the 4-3-3, **Fernandinho (25)** would therefore take up a position between the 2 attacking midfielders to find space and receive.

Switching Play to the Weak Side After Stretching the Opposition's Defence (Against the 4-3-3)

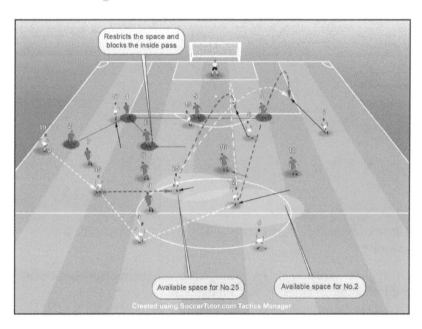

The winger **(19)** passes back to the full back **(35)**, as the inside pass is blocked. The ball is either passed to the defensive midfielder **(25)** or moved to the other full back **(2)** via the centre back **(5)**.

The defensive midfielder **(25)** or the full back **(2)** receive and switch play to the weak side with a long pass to the attacking midfielder **(8)** or the winger **(7)**, depending on the gap between the red centre back (No.5) and full back (No.3).

NOTE:
The training session (5 practices) in "Tactical Situation 7: Stretching the Opposition's Defence and Switching Play (Against the 4-4-2 or the 4-2-3-1)" can be adjusted to play against the 4-3-3 formation - see the passing options in the diagram above.

TACTICAL SITUATION 11

Switching Play to the Weak Side when the Overload is Blocked Against the 4-3-3

Content from Analysis of Manchester City during the 2017/2018 and 2018/2019 Premier League winning seasons

The analysis is based on recurring patterns of play observed within the Manchester City team. Once the same phase of play occurred a number of times (at least 10) the tactics would be seen as a pattern. The analysis on the next page is an example of the team's tactics being used effectively, taken from a specific game.

Each action, pass, individual movement with or without the ball, and the positioning of each player on the pitch including their body shape, are presented.

The analysis is then used to create a full progressive session to coach this specific tactical situation.

AVAILABLE SPACES TO MOVE THE BALL WHEN THE OVERLOAD IS BLOCKED AGAINST THE 4-3-3

Available Spaces to Exploit on the Weak Side when the Opposition Block the Overload on the Strong Side (Against the 4-3-3)

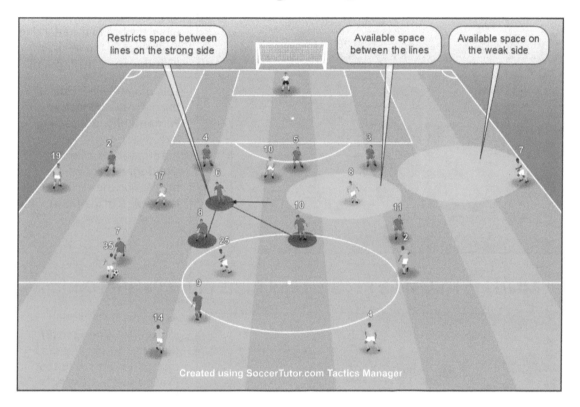

When playing against the 4-3-3, the opposing defensive midfielder (red No.6) controlled the Manchester City attacking midfielder on the strong side **(De Bruyne - 17 in diagram)**.

This meant that the potential 2v1 advantage within the zone of responsibility of the opposing full back (red No.2) was not possible and is blocked by the opposition.

The opposing defensive midfielder (red No.6) shifts across to control the City attacking midfielder **De Bruyne (17)** and block the potential 2v1 overload from being created.

Even if **De Bruyne (17)** managed to receive and turn, he would be closed down by red No.6 and the red team would retain their balance.

However, this positioning left space in specific areas where City could create a favourable situation - see available space between the lines and on the weak side in the diagram.

There is a 2v1 overload with the other attacking midfielder **Gündoğan (8)** and the winger **Sterling (7)** on the weak side against the red full back No.3, so Manchester City's aim is to play to either of them.

PEP GUARDIOLA'S ATTACKING TACTICS

MOVING THE BALL TO THE **ATTACKING MIDFIELDER** ON THE WEAK SIDE

1. Moving the Ball to the Attacking Midfielder on the Weak Side

Pep Guardiola's Manchester City team use quick passing to move the ball to the attacking midfielder on the weak side **(Gündoğan - 8 in diagram)**.

This was achieved with the defensive midfielder **Fernandinho (25)** passing directly (diagonal) to the attacking midfielder **Gündoğan (8)** or via the full back on the weak side **(Walker - 2 in diagram)**, who shifts across to receive.

2. Attacking Midfielder Receives and Turns with 2 Passing Options

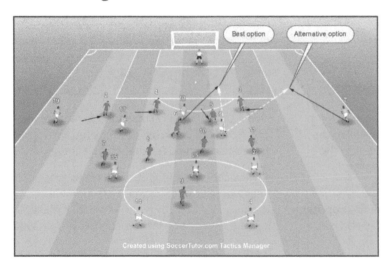

As soon as the attacking midfielder **Gündoğan (8)** receives, he turns free of marking, as the red full back (No.3) also has the winger **Sterling (7)** within his zone of responsibility.

Gündoğan (8) has 2 available passing options - the pass to the forward **Agüero (10)** is the most likely to result in a City goal.

If red No.3 did move to put pressure on **Gündoğan (8)**, the ball would be moved to the free player **Sterling (7)** directly if possible, or via the full back **Walker (2)**.

SWITCHING PLAY TO THE WINGER ON THE WEAK SIDE (IN A WIDE POSITION)

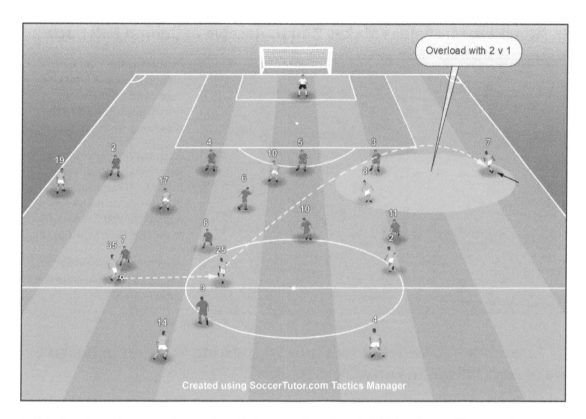

Overload with 2 v 1

Created using SoccerTutor.com Tactics Manager

In this situation, a long pass is used to switch play to the winger on the weak side **(Sterling - 7 in diagram)**.

Together with the attacking midfielder on the weak side **(Gündoğan - 8 in diagram)**, this creates a 2v1 overload in the opposing full back's (red No.3) zone of responsibility.

Pep Guardiola's Manchester City team then use specific movements which depend on:

1. The positioning of the opposing defenders.

2. The area the ball is received by the winger (wide or narrow).

ATTACKING MIDFIELDER SUPPORTS THE WINGER AFTER SWITCH OF PLAY TO A WIDE POSITION

1. Attacking Midfielder Makes Run to Receive in Behind Full Back

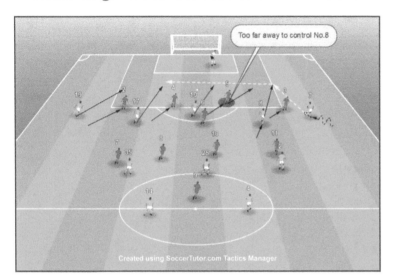

As soon as the switch of play is made, the attacking midfielder on the weak side **(Gündoğan - 8 in the diagram)** reads the situation.

As the opposing centre back (red No.5) is too far away to control **Gündoğan (8)**, he makes a diagonal run in behind the red full back (No.3) to receive from **Sterling (7)**.

After receiving, **Gündoğan (8)** delivers a low cross into the penalty area.

2. Attacking Midfielder Moves into Supporting Position to Receive Back and Deliver an Early Cross

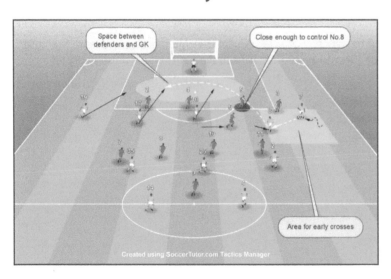

In this variation of the previous example, the opposing centre back (red No.5) is now close enough to control City's attacking midfielder on the weak side **(Gündoğan - 8 in the diagram)**.

Gündoğan (8) stays in a supporting position for the right winger **Sterling (7)** and receives the pass back. The City attacking midfielder in this position usually delivers an early cross into the space between the defenders and goalkeeper.

PEP GUARDIOLA'S ATTACKING TACTICS

FULL BACK SUPPORTS THE WINGER AFTER SWITCH OF PLAY TO A WIDE POSITION

1. Full Back Moves Forward to Support the Winger when the Attacking Midfielder is Unable to Create an Overload Wide

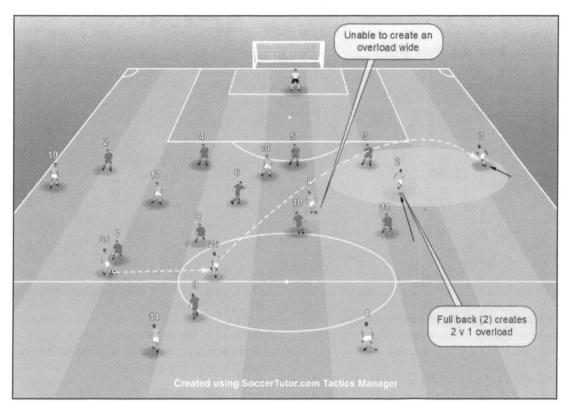

When the attacking midfielder on the weak side **(Gündoğan - 8 in diagram example)** was in a more central position and unable to create an overload wide, Pep Guardiola's Manchester City team instead try to create a favourable 2v1 overload on the weak side with the forward movement of the full back **(Walker - 2 in diagram)**.

The Manchester City full back on the weak side **Walker (2)** notices the attacking midfielder **Gündoğan (8)** is unable to create an overload wide. He therefore moves into an advanced position as soon as the switch of play is made by the defensive midfielder **Fernandinho (25)**.

This forward movement of the full back **Walker (2)** creates a 2v1 situation together with the Manchester City right winger **Sterling (7)** against the opposing full back (red No3).

2. Opposing Centre Back is Too Far Away to Track Runs in Behind: Full Back Makes Underlapping Run to Receive

Created using SoccerTutor.com Tactics Manager

Manchester City's next movements depend on the positioning of the red centre back on that side (No.5 in diagram example).

If the opposing centre back (red No.5) was too far away to control the movement of the City full back **Walker (2)** or decided to stay in a central position to defend a potential cross, then **Walker (2)** would make an underlapping run, as shown.

The opposing full back (red No.3) has to close down the City winger **Sterling (7)**, so the right back **Walker (2)** is free to make an underlapping run and receive in behind red No.3.

From this point, **Walker (2)** is in a favourable position to deliver a cross for his team-mates.

NOTE:

The underlapping run was more frequently used by **Walker (2)** on the right, as the Manchester City right back has the speed that **Delph (18)** and **Zinchenko (35)** don't have on the left.

On the left, **Delph (18)** and **Zinchenko (35)** have the qualities of midfielders, so they are better at playing key/final passes, delivering early crosses and sometimes overlapping, rather than underlapping runs.

3. Opposing Centre Back is Closer and Able to Track Runs in Behind: Full Back Supports, Receives Back and Delivers an Early Cross

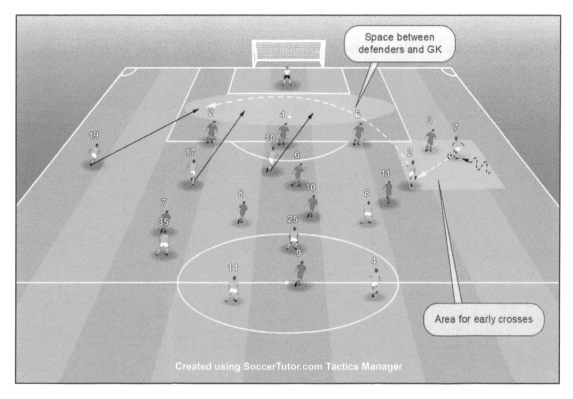

If the opposing centre back (red No.5) was close enough to the Manchester City right back **Walker (2)**, he could then control the potential underlapping run and any run into the space behind the full back (red No.3).

Therefore, **Walker (2)** decides to remain in a supporting position and receive the pass back from the City winger **Sterling (7)** within the early crossing area (yellow highlighted area in the diagram).

Walker (2) delivers an early cross into the space between the defenders and the goalkeeper (white highlighted area) for his team-mates **(10, 17 & 19)** to run onto and try to score.

SWITCHING PLAY TO THE WINGER WHO MOVES INSIDE **(IN A NARROW POSITION)**

Winger Moves Inside to Receive a Long Switch of Play in a Narrow Position

Winger receives in a narrow position

Created using SoccerTutor.com Tactics Manager

If the long pass was received in a narrower position (the winger moves more inside), the Manchester City players used different options to break through the opposition's defence, compared to when the winger received in a wider position (see previous 3 pages).

In this example, the City right winger **Sterling (7)** receives the long pass (switch of play) from the defensive midfielder **Fernandinho (25)** in a position closer to the centre.

When receiving in a narrower position, the opposing centre back (red No.5) is able to control the City attacking midfielder on the weak side **(Gündoğan - 8 in diagram example)** much easier.

The potential run in behind from **Gündoğan (8)** was also easier to defend because the full back (red No.3) didn't have to move too wide, thus creating a smaller gap and less space to exploit.

ATTACKING MIDFIELDER SUPPORTS THE WINGER AFTER SWITCH OF PLAY TO A NARROW POSITION

1. Attacking Midfielder's Overlapping Run to Receive in Behind

The options for City to break through the defence are different when the winger receives in a narrower position.

The attacking midfielder **Gündoğan (8)** makes an overlapping run to exploit the space out wide and a 2v1 situation against the full back (red No.3).

2. Opposing Full Back Tracks Attacking Midfielder's Overlapping Run: Winger Has Space to Deliver Early Cross

This is a variation of the previous example, with the opposing full back (red No.3) tracking **Gündoğan's (8)** run to prevent the 2v1.

However, the winger **Sterling (7)** stays free of marking for a couple of seconds and is able to deliver an early cross into the space between the defenders and the goalkeeper.

PEP GUARDIOLA'S ATTACKING TACTICS

FULL BACK SUPPORTS THE WINGER AFTER SWITCH OF PLAY TO A NARROW POSITION

1. Full Back's Overlapping Run to Receive in Behind

Created using SoccerTutor.com Tactics Manager

The full back **Walker (2)** makes an overlapping run to exploit the space out wide and exploit a 2v1 situation against the opposing full back (red No.3).

Manchester City exploit this situation in one of the following ways:

1. The winger passes to the full back **Walker (2)**, who receives on the run and crosses for his **team-mates** (as shown in the diagram above).

2. If the opposing full back (red No.3) tracks **Walker's (2)** run, the winger Sterling (7) has time and space to deliver an early cross (see diagram on the next page).

2. Opposing Full Back Tracks Full Back's Overlapping Run: Winger Has Space to Deliver an Early Cross

Created using SoccerTutor.com Tactics Manager

This is a variation of the previous example, with the opposing full back (red No.3) tracking **Walker's (2)** run to prevent the 2v1.

However, the winger **Sterling (7)** stays free of marking for a couple of seconds and is able to deliver an early cross into the space between the defenders and the goalkeeper.

NOTE:

All the situations in this section are presented against the 4-3-3, but these same situations also occur for Manchester City against the 4-4-2 and 4-2-3-1.

Against the 4-4-2 and 4-2-3-1, these situations are created if the opposition block the overload or if all the opposing players shift towards the strong side and space is limited around the ball area.

Switching Play to the Weak Side when the Overload is Blocked Against the 4-3-3

Practice 1: Switching Play to the Winger on the Weak Side in a Functional Practice (vs Full Back)

Scenario A: Winger Receives in a Wide Position and the Attacking Midfielder Makes an Underlapping Run

Created using SoccerTutor.com Tactics Manager

Objective: Switching play to the winger on the weak side to create and exploit a 2v1 overload.

Description (Scenario A)

There are 2 wide zones which are 12 x 5 yards divided in half (yellow wide and blue narrow).

There are also 2 white central zones, which are 8 x 7 yards for the blue attacking midfielders (**17 & 8**) and the red full backs (No.2 & No.3).

The practice starts with the centre back (**14**) passing to the defensive midfielder (**25**), who lays the ball back. The centre back (**14**) then passes to the full back (**35**), who has dropped back to receive.

The full back (**35**) moves forward with the ball and then passes to the defensive midfielder (**25**).

The defensive midfielder (**25**) switches play to the winger (**7**) on the weak side.

In Scenario A, the winger (**7**) receives in a wide position (<u>inside the yellow zone</u>), so the attacking midfielder (**8**) makes an **underlapping run** to receive behind the red full back (No.3).

From there, the attacking midfielder (**8**) delivers a low cross for oncoming team-mates to finish.

The practice restarts with the pattern carried out on the opposite side.

PEP GUARDIOLA'S ATTACKING TACTICS

Scenario B: Winger Receives in a Narrow Position and the Attacking Midfielder Makes an Overlapping Run

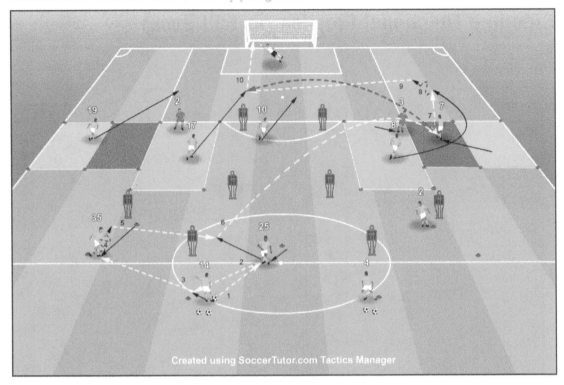

Created using SoccerTutor.com Tactics Manager

Description (Scenario B)

This variation again shows the defensive midfielder **(25)** switching play to the winger **(7)** on the weak side.

In Scenario B, the winger **(7)** receives in a narrow position (<u>inside the blue zone</u>), so the attacking midfielder **(8)** makes an **overlapping run** to receive in behind the red full back (No.3).

From there, the attacking midfielder **(8)** delivers a low cross for oncoming team-mates to finish.

However, if the opposing full back (red No.3) tracks the overlapping run of the blue attacking midfielder **(8)**, the winger **(7)** will have time and space to deliver an early cross into the space between the defenders and the goalkeeper - see the blue arrow in the diagram example.

The practice restarts with the pattern carried out on the opposite side.

Scenario C: Winger Receives in a Wide Position and the Full Back Makes an Underlapping Run

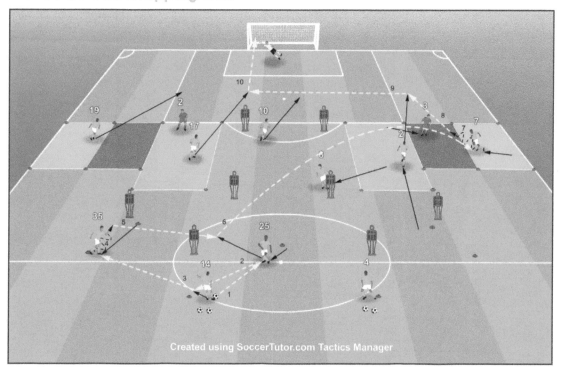

Created using SoccerTutor.com Tactics Manager

Description (Scenario C)

This variation shows what happens when the attacking midfielder **(8)** is in a more central position and unable to create a 2v1 overload on the weak side.

In this practice, the attacking midfielder **(8)** drops back and out of the white zone. As soon as the defensive midfielder plays the long pass (switch of play), the full back on the weak side **(2)** moves forward into the white zone, as shown.

For Scenario C, the winger **(7)** receives in a wide position (inside the yellow zone), so the full back **(2)** makes an **underlapping run** to receive behind the red full back (No.3).

From there, the full back **(2)** delivers a low cross for oncoming team-mates to finish.

The practice restarts with the pattern carried out on the opposite side.

Scenario D: Winger Receives in a Narrow Position and the Full Back Makes an Overlapping Run

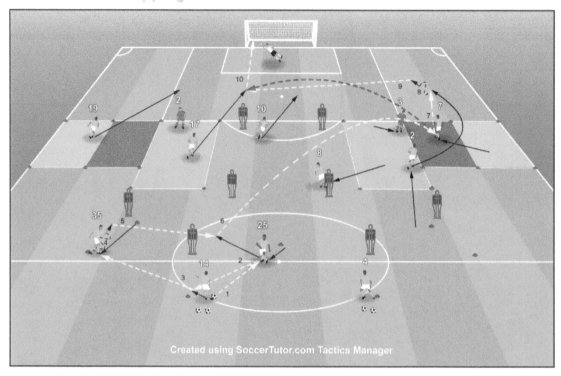

Created using SoccerTutor.com Tactics Manager

Description (Scenario D)

In Scenario D, the winger **(7)** receives in a narrow position (<u>inside the blue zone</u>), so the full back **(2)** makes an **overlapping run** to receive in behind the opposing full back (red No.3).

From there, the full back **(2)** delivers a low cross for oncoming team-mates to finish.

However, if the opposing full back (red No.3) tracks the overlapping run of the blue full back **(2)**, the winger **(7)** will have time and space to deliver an early cross into the space between the defenders and the goalkeeper - see the blue arrow in the diagram example.

The practice restarts with the pattern carried out on the opposite side.

Coaching Points

1. Read the tactical situation: The blue attacking midfielder or full back must notice the area the winger receives the ball (wide or narrow) and the positioning of the closest red centre back (No.5).

2. Well-timed runs of the players e.g. the blue full back takes advantage of the transmission phase (time the ball takes to travel) to move forward and create/exploit a 2v1 overload.

PROGRESSION

Practice 2: Switching Play to the Winger on the Weak Side in a Functional Practice (vs Back 4)

Scenario A: Opposing Centre Back is Close and Able to Track Runs in Behind the Full Back

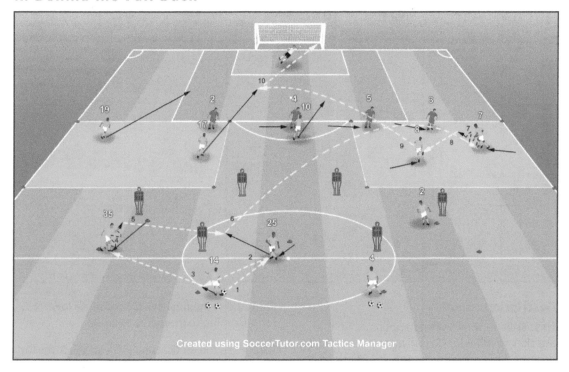

Created using SoccerTutor.com Tactics Manager

Objective: Switching play to the winger on the weak side to create and exploit a 2v1 overload.

Description (Scenario A)

The is a progression of the previous practice. There are 2 wide zones for the 2v1 overload after a switch of play.

The blue players carry out the same passing pattern and as soon as the defensive midfielder **(25)** switches play, the players have to read the tactical situation and exploit the overload in the best possible way.

The first important factor is where the winger **(7)** receives the ball. Please see the tactical analysis

and practices for all possible situations, reactions and options.

The second important factor is the positioning of the closest centre back (red No.5).

In Scenario A, the winger **(7)** receives in a wide position and the opposing centre back (red No.5) is close enough to control any runs behind the full back (red No.3).

The attacking midfielder **(8)** therefore stays in a supporting position to receive back from the winger **(7)** and deliver an early cross into the space between the defenders and the goalkeeper.

Scenario B: Opposing Centre Back is Too Far Away to Track Runs in Behind the Full Back

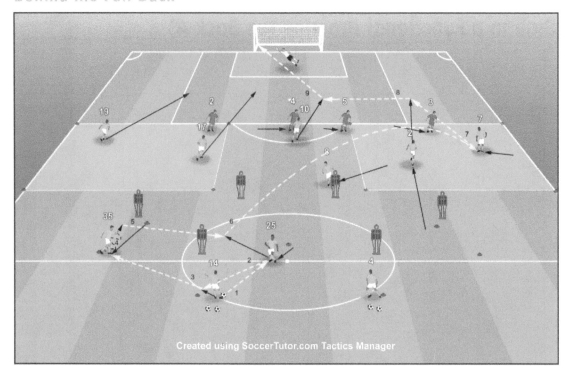

Created using SoccerTutor.com Tactics Manager

Description (Scenario B)

This variation shows what happens when the attacking midfielder **(8)** is in a more central position and unable to create a 2v1 overload on the weak side.

In this practice, the attacking midfielder **(8)** drops back and out of the <u>white zone</u>. As soon as the defensive midfielder plays the long pass (switch of play), the full back on the weak side **(2)** moves forward into the <u>white zone</u>, as shown.

In Scenario B, the red centre back (No.5) is too far away to track runs in behind the red full back (No.3). He is outside the <u>white zone</u>.

In this example, the winger **(7)** has received in a wide position, so the blue full back **(2)** makes an **underlapping run** to receive in behind the red full back (No.3).

From there, the full back **(2)** delivers a low cross for oncoming team-mates to finish.

Please see the tactical analysis and practices for all possible situations, reactions and options.

The practice restarts with the pattern carried out on the opposite side.

Coaching Points

1. Read the tactical situation: The blue attacking midfielder or full back must notice the area the winger receives the ball (wide or narrow) and the positioning of the closest red centre back (No.5).

2. Well-timed runs of the players e.g. the blue full back takes advantage of the transmission phase (time the ball takes to travel) to move forward and create/exploit a 2v1 overload.

PROGRESSION

Practice 3: Switching Play to the Winger on the Weak Side in a Dynamic Conditioned Game

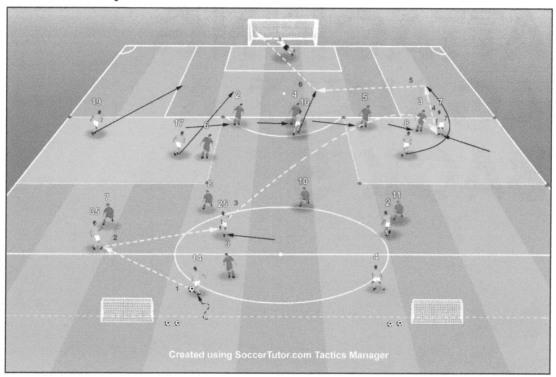

Created using SoccerTutor.com Tactics Manager

Description

This is a progression of the previous practice, moving into a 10 v 10 (+GK) game. The blue team start the practice with the centre back **(14)** from the end line.

The blue team can score in any way (1 point), but if they score after switching play and exploiting the overload wide on the weak side, they score 2 points.

Please see the tactical analysis and practices for all possible situations, reactions and options.

If the reds win possession, they try to score in either mini goal within 10-12 seconds (2 points).

Coaching Points

1. Read the tactical situation: The blue attacking midfielder or full back must notice the area the winger receives the ball (wide or narrow) and the positioning of the closest red centre back (No.5).

2. Well-timed runs of the players e.g. the blue full back takes advantage of the transmission phase (time the ball takes to travel) to move forward and create/exploit a 2v1 overload.

Progression

11v11 game in 2/3 of the pitch with the same aims and but without any marked out zones.

ATTACKING AGAINST A BACK 5

TACTICAL SITUATION 12

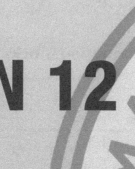

Attacking Against a Back 5

Content from Analysis of Manchester City during the 2017/2018 and 2018/2019 Premier League winning seasons

The analysis is based on recurring patterns of play observed within the Manchester City team. Once the same phase of play occurred a number of times (at least 10) the tactics would be seen as a pattern. The analysis on the next page is an example of the team's tactics being used effectively, taken from a specific game.

Each action, pass, individual movement with or without the ball, and the positioning of each player on the pitch including their body shape, are presented.

The analysis is then used to create a full progressive session to coach this specific tactical situation.

THE ATTACKING LIMITATIONS WHEN PLAYING AGAINST A BACK 5

1. How a Back 5 Formation Blocks the Overload in Both Wide Areas

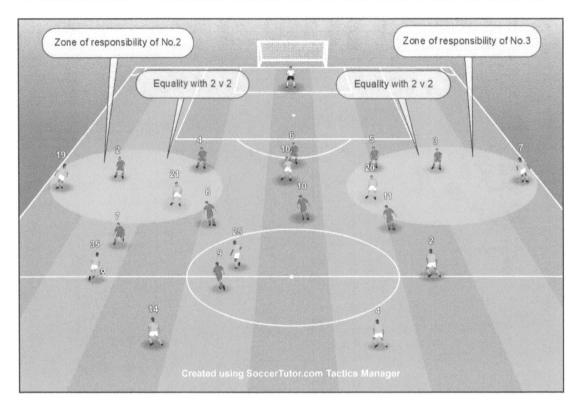

As Pep Guardiola's attacking tactics rely a lot on exploiting the overload wide, this forces many opposing coaches to use a formation with 5 players at the back when playing against Manchester City.

This means there is an extra defender and the opponents can control the Manchester City attacking midfielders on both sides.

The example above shows the opposition using the 5-4-1 formation and there is a 2v2 equality of numbers in both wide areas.

This meant that the Manchester City attacking midfielders **(21 & 20 in diagram example)** could not receive in between the lines and turn towards the opponent's goal as easily, so the team could not create 2v1 overloads in wide areas.

2. Reactions of the Opposition's Back 5 to Prevent Manchester City from Breaking Through their Defence

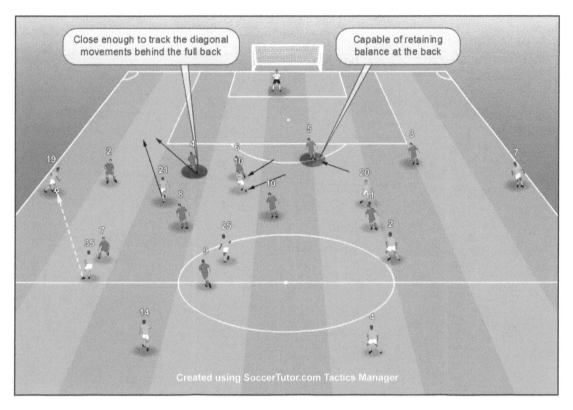

The opposition's wide centre backs (red No.4 and No.5) are close enough to track the diagonal runs of Manchester City's attacking midfielders **(21 & 20)** in behind the wing backs (red No.2 and No.3).

In this example, as soon as the ball is directed to the left winger **Sané (19)**, the attacking midfielder **Silva (21)** makes a diagonal run in behind the opposing right wing back (red No.2).

As shown in the diagram example, the red right centre back (No.4) is close enough to track the run of City's attacking midfielder **Silva (21)**, so this passing option is blocked.

This reaction widens the inside passing lane and the City forward **Agüero (10)** makes a movement to provide a passing option.

However, the opposing centre back on the weak side (red No.5) is capable of retaining balance at the back by shifting across to the centre, so if the City winger **Sané (19)** attempts an inside pass, the middle centre back (red No.6) can move forward and restrict the space available for **Agüero (10)**, as shown in the diagram.

NOTE: This reaction from the opposition is not possible when they play with a back 4.

PEP GUARDIOLA'S ATTACKING TACTICS

3. The Opposing Wide Centre Back Prevents the Attacking Midfielder from Receiving and Turning Between the Lines

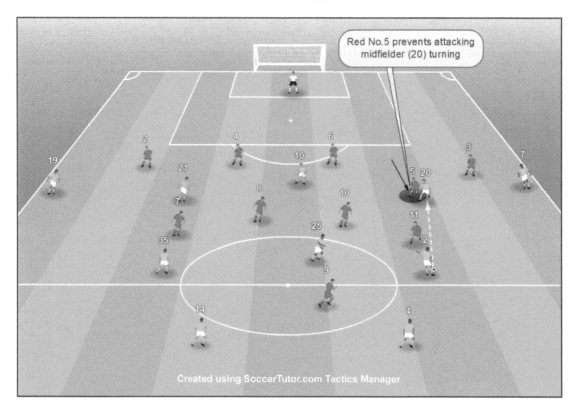

Red No.5 prevents attacking midfielder (20) turning

Created using SoccerTutor.com Tactics Manager

As there is an equality of numbers (2v2) in wide areas, it becomes much harder for the Manchester City attacking midfielders to receive between the lines and turn to face the opponent's goal.

The opposing full back (red No.3 in diagram) is marking the Manchester City winger **(Sterling - 7 in diagram example)** and the opposing wide centre back (red No.5) is free to control the attacking midfielder **Bernardo (20)**.

If a pass is played to the attacking midfielder between the lines **Bernardo (20)**, the red centre back (No.5) can move forward to mark him closely and prevent him from turning.

Manchester City are unable to advance their attack and **Bernardo (20)** would most likely just try to maintain possession for his team in this situation.

NOTE:

Pep Guardiola's Manchester City have solutions for these attacking limitations when playing against a back 5, which have been displayed on these 3 pages.

These attacking solutions are shown in the analysis and session on the pages to follow.

RECEIVING IN BEHIND THE OPPOSING WING BACK

1. The Winger Attacks the Space in Behind the Wing Back when Closely Marked

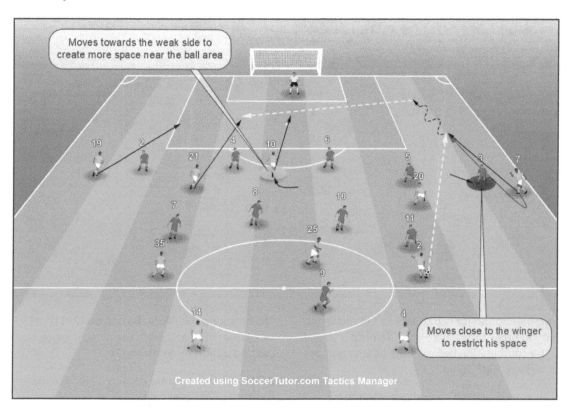

As shown on the previous page, it is unlikely that the attacking midfielder **(Bernardo - 20 in diagram example)** can receive and turn between the lines, so Manchester City instead focus on playing the ball to the winger.

Manchester City use different options to play the ball in behind to the winger **(Sterling - 7 in diagram example)**, depending on the positioning of the opposing wing back (red No3).

If the red No3 is close enough to restrict **Sterling's (7)** space or even prevent him from

receiving facing the goal, then the winger attacked the space in behind him.

This action was either carried out with an initial dropping back movement, followed by a sudden change of direction (as shown in the diagram example) or simply a sudden forward run.

In addition, the City forward **Agüero (10)** moves towards the weak side to drag his marker (red No.6) with him and create more space near the ball area.

2. 1-2 Combination Out Wide to Receive Behind the Wing Back

Moves towards the weak side to create more space near the ball area

Marks No.20 goal side

Created using SoccerTutor.com Tactics Manager

Another option for Pep Guardiola's Manchester City to break through a 5-man defence is to use a 1-2 combination between the winger and the attacking midfielder.

This combination is carried out when the opposing wing back isn't close enough to the City winger, who is able to receive facing the opponent's goal.

This example shows **Sterling (7)** receiving from the full back **Walker (2)**.

The attacking midfielder **Bernardo (20)** checks away from his marker and moves to provide a passing option for **Sterling (7)**.

As the opposing centre back (red No.5) marks **Bernardo (20)** goal-side, a 1-2 combination can be played so that **Sterling (7)** can receive in behind the wing back (red No.3) and deliver a low cross for oncoming team-mates.

NOTE:

Manchester City often use the 1-2 combination in these situations, but they also use the give-and-go in wide areas to break through the opposition's defence.

Please see "Tactical Situation 6: Combination Play Out Wide when the Overload is Blocked."

PEP GUARDIOLA'S ATTACKING TACTICS

3. Attacking Midfielder Drops Back to Create Space and then Quickly Runs in Behind to Receive in Behind

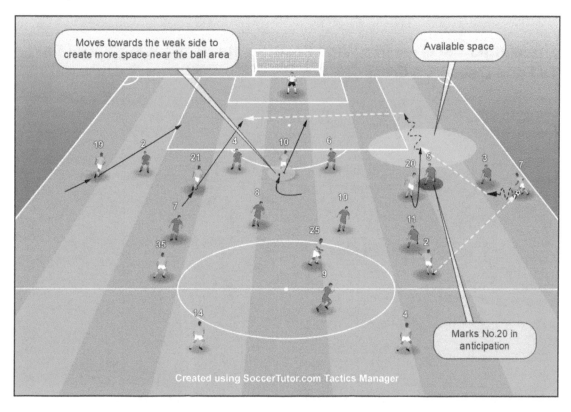

In this variation of the previous example, the red centre back (No.5) is able to mark City's attacking midfielder **Bernardo (20)** tightly and prevent him from receiving. However, available space is created behind the red centre back (No.5), which can be exploited by **Bernardo (20)**.

The winger **Sterling (7)** moves inside with the ball to find an available passing lane and **Bernardo (20)** drops back, before quickly changing direction and running into the available space created in behind.

Sterling (7) times his pass in behind for **Bernardo (20)** to run onto. **Bernardo (20)** receives, dribbles forward and crosses.

Agüero (10) again moves towards the weak side to drag his marker (red No.6) with him and create more space near the ball area.

SWITCHING PLAY TO THE WEAK SIDE AND ISOLATING THE WING BACK IN A 1v1 SITUATION

The Winger Receives in a Wide Position, Beats the Wing Back in a 1v1 and Delivers a Cross

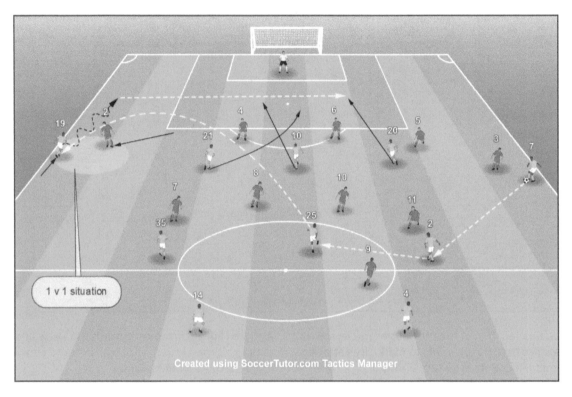

Pep Guardiola's Manchester City also use this simple but effective tactical movement to break through a 5-man defence.

The ball is directed to the winger on the weak side in order to take advantage of the ability of **Sané (19)**, **Sterling (7)**, **Bernardo (20)** or **Mahrez (26)** to beat their opponents in 1v1 duels and deliver crosses for their team-mates.

In this example, the defensive midfielder **Fernandinho (25)** switches play to **Sané (19)**, who beats the red wing back (No.2) on the outside, dribbles forward and delivers a low cross for **Bernardo (20)** to finish.

SWITCHING PLAY TO THE WEAK SIDE, CREATING A 2v1 OVERLOAD AND DELIVERING AN EARLY CROSS

Full Back Moves Forward to Provide Support for the Winger and Deliver an Early Cross Against a 5-Man Defence

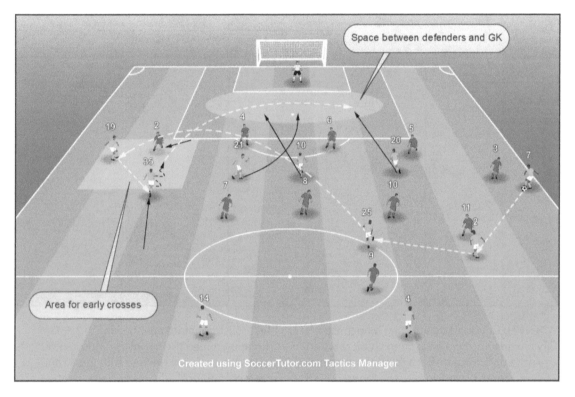

Pep Guardiola's Manchester City also use early crosses to create scoring chances against a 5-man defence.

The crosses were either delivered by the full back, the attacking midfielder or even the winger when there was a rotation between the 3 wide players.

In this example, the full back **Zinchenko (35)** moves forward as soon as the defensive midfielder **Fernandinho (25)** switches play.

This creates a 2v1 overload and **Zinchenko (35)** is able to receive a pass back from **Sané (19)**, and then deliver an early cross into the space between the defenders and the goalkeeper.

SWITCHING TO A 2-2-5-1 FORMATION:
CREATING 2v1 SITUATIONS OUT WIDE

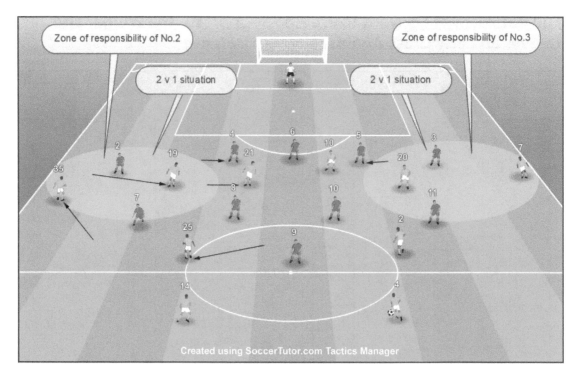

Zone of responsibility of No.2

Zone of responsibility of No.3

2 v 1 situation

2 v 1 situation

Created using SoccerTutor.com Tactics Manager

When Pep Guardiola notices that Manchester City are unable to create scoring chances when against a back 5, he makes a tactical switch by adding 1 more player close to the forward.

Either the attacking midfielder or the winger shift towards the centre to play close to the forward. In the diagram example, this is the attacking midfielder **Silva (21)**. The other player **(the winger Sané - 19 in this example)** moves towards the inside as well.

At the same time, the respective full back moves into a wide position to provide width **(Zinchenko - 35 in this example)**. To retain balance, the defensive midfielder **Fernandinho (25)** moves towards the left and the right back **Walker (2)** moves towards the centre to complete the new 2-2-5-1 formation.

This adjustment into an attacking 2-2-5-1 formation forced the opposing wide centre backs (red No.4 and No.5) to shift inside and create a numerical advantage in the centre.

As red No.4 and No.5 have moved into more central positions, there is a 2v1 situation in both wide areas.

Manchester City tried to exploit these potential 2v1 overloads in the same way as they did against a 4-man defence - see "Tactical Situation 3: Creating and Exploiting Overloads in Wide Areas."

SWITCHING TO A 2-2-5-1 FORMATION:
ATTACKING THROUGH THE CENTRE

1. Attacking Midfielder Receives in the Centre and Turns Unmarked

Created using SoccerTutor.com Tactics Manager

If the opposing wide centre backs (red No.4 and No.5) take up wider positions to prevent the 2v1 overloads in wide areas, Pep Guardiola's Manchester City team then attack through the centre.

The attacking midfielders have moved inside to take up positions in the centre of the pitch. This often leads to a 4v3 numerical advantage in the central area.

The main aim for Manchester City is to pass to an attacking midfielder in between the lines, so they can receive, turn facing the goal and play a final pass in behind.

As soon as **Walker (2)** passes to the defensive midfielder **Fernandinho (25)**, the attacking midfielder positioned close to the forward in the centre **(Silva - 21 in diagram example)** moves into an available passing lane to receive.

If the opposing defender (red No.4) doesn't move to close him down, **Silva (21)** receives and turns in a crucial area to find a key/final pass for the run of one of his team-mates.

2. Attacking Midfielder is Unable to Receive in the Centre and Moves the Ball to a Free Player to Play a Final Pass

Available space

In this variation, the attacking midfielder **Silva (21)** is closed down by the opposing centre back (red No.4).

Silva (21) plays a first time pass to the other attacking midfielder **Bernardo (20)** - the free player.

Bernardo (20) can then play a key/final pass to **No.19** who exploits the available space behind red No.4 or into the path of **No.10** or **No.7**.

3. Forward Drops Back to Receive and Move the Ball to a Free Player to Play a Final Pass

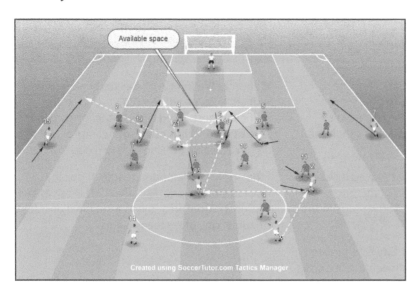

Available space

When there is no available passing lane to the attacking midfielder **Silva (21)**, the forward **Agüero (10)** drops back to receive.

He can either turn and pass if he is unmarked, or pass to the free player if he is closed down (as shown in the diagram).

Silva (21) receives facing the opponent's goal in a crucial area to find a key/final pass for the run of one of his team-mates.

Attacking Against a Back 5

Practice 1: Attacking Out Wide or Through the Centre Against a Back 5 in a Functional Practice

Scenario A: The Full Back Receives and the Opposing Centre Back is Too Far Away to Track the Winger's Run in Behind the Wing Back

Created using SoccerTutor.com Tactics Manager

Description (Scenario A)

There are 2 <u>yellow wide zones</u> where a 2v1 overload is created and a <u>central white zone</u>. There are 5 mannequins representing the 4 red midfielders and 1 forward in the 5-4-1 formation.

The blue team are in Pep Guardiola's 2-2-5-1 attacking formation.

The 2 blue centre backs **(14 & 4)** pass the ball to each other and as soon as one of them receives and turns **(14 in diagram)**, the 2 players in midfield **(25 & 2)** move to receive.

The blue centre back **(14)** can either pass the ball wide to the advanced full back **(35)** or centrally.

In Scenario A, the ball is passed to the advanced full back **(35)** in the <u>yellow wide zone</u> and there is an attempt to exploit the 2v1 overload. The full back **(35)** must make the best possible decision about where to play the next pass, depending on the reaction of the opposing defenders.

In the diagram example, the opposing right centre back (red No.4) is too far away to track the run of the blue winger **(19)**. Therefore, he makes a run in behind the red wing back No.2, receives and crosses into the penalty area.

Please see all the tactical analysis and all practices in this session for all the possible defensive reactions and attacking options.

Scenario B: The Full Back Receives and the Opposing Centre Back Tracks the Winger's Run in Behind the Wing Back

Created using SoccerTutor.com Tactics Manager

Description (Scenario B)

In Scenario B, the red centre back (No.4) tracks the run of the blue winger **(19)**.

As the full back **(35)** is closed down, he passes back to the defensive midfielder **(25)**.

From this point, the defensive midfielder **(25)** switches play with a long pass. He must make the decision about where to play the pass.

In the diagram example, the defensive midfielder **(25)** switches play to the winger on the weak side **(7)**, who can receive unmarked as all the red defenders have shifted across.

If there was a gap between the defenders to exploit, the defensive midfielder **(25)** would look to play a long pass into a central area.

Please see all the tactical analysis and all practices in this session for all the possible defensive reactions and attacking options.

Coaching Points

1. Quality high speed passing (1 or 2 touches).
2. Quality low crosses and finishing.
3. Well synchronised movements of the players.

Scenario C: Attacking Midfielder Receives in the Centre and Opposing Centre Back Closes Him Down

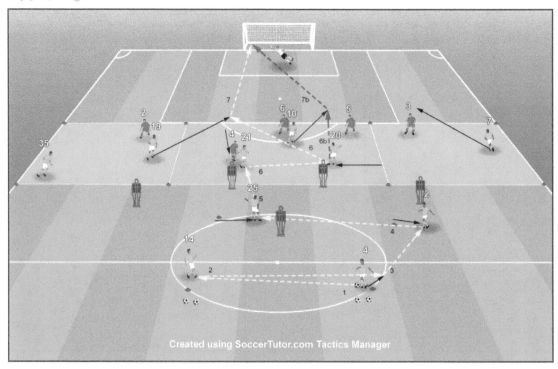

Created using SoccerTutor.com Tactics Manager

Description (Scenario C)

In Scenario C, the defensive midfielder **(25)** passes into the <u>central white zone</u>.

One of the central players **(No.21 in diagram)** moves to into a passing lane to receive. The options depend on the reaction of the opposing defender (red No.4):

1. If red No.4 doesn't move to close blue **No.21** down, he receives and turns in a crucial area to find a key/final pass for the run of one of his team-mates.

2. If red No.4 follows blue **No.21**, he plays a first time pass to the other attacking midfielder **No.20** (the free player). **No.20** then plays a key/final pass for the run of one of his team-mates - see diagram example.

The defensive midfielder **(25)** can pass to either attacking midfielder **(21 or 20)** or the forward **(10)**, who can drop back to receive.

Please see all the tactical analysis and all practices in this session for all the possible defensive reactions and attacking options.

Coaching Points

1. Decision making according to the reaction of the opposing defenders.

2. Exploiting the overload wide.

3. Receiving and turning quickly.

4. Using passing combinations to move the ball to the free player in the centre.

PROGRESSION

Practice 2: Attacking Options Against a Back 5 in a Dynamic Game

Created using SoccerTutor.com Tactics Manager

Description

In this progression, the blues start the game with the centre back **(4)** from the end line.

1. At first, the blue team try to attack the reds and score by exploiting the 2v1 overload in wide areas (<u>within yellow zones</u>).

2. If the red team react properly and block the overload e.g. the wide centre back (red No.4 in diagram) tracks the run of the blue winger **No.19**, they then try to score after quickly switching play - see diagram example.

3. There is also always the possibility to attack through the centre, especially if the opposing centre backs No.4 and No.5 are in wider positions - attacking options for this are shown in Scenario C of the previous practice.

If the reds win possession, they try to score in either mini goal within 10-12 seconds (2 points).

The marked zones are only used to make it easier for the blues to read the tactical situation and can be removed.

Coaching Points

1. Decision making according to the reaction of the opposing defenders.

2. Exploiting the overload wide.

3. Receiving and turning quickly.

4. Using passing combinations to move the ball to the free player in the centre.

PROGRESSION

Practice 3: Attacking Against a Back 5 in an 11v11 Conditioned Game

Created using SoccerTutor.com Tactics Manager

Description

In this final practice of the session, the 2 teams play a conditioned 11v11 game. The practice starts from the blue team's goalkeeper.

The blue team can score in any way (1 point), but if they score in any of the following ways, they score 2 points.

1. Exploiting 2v1 overload in a wide area.

2. Switch play when the overload is blocked.

3. Attack through the centre by receiving and turning between the lines or using a passing combination to move the ball to the free player, as shown in the diagram example.

Please see all the tactical analysis and all practices in this session for all the possible defensive reactions and attacking options.

Coaching Points

1. Decision making according to the reaction of the opposing defenders.

2. Exploiting the overload wide.

3. Receiving and turning quickly.

4. Using passing combinations to move the ball to the free player in the centre.

Football Coaching Specialists Since 2001

PEP GUARDIOLA

Practices Direct from Pep's Training Sessions at Man City, Bayern Munich and FC Barcelona

4 players make runs into the penalty area

All players jog back to their positions (no walking)

Created using SoccerTutor.com Tactics Manager

Printed in June 2019
by Rotomail Italia S.p.A., Vignate (MI) - Italy